THIS IS
WENDELL WILLKIE

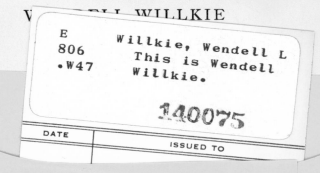

WENDELL WILLKIE

THIS IS
WENDELL
WILLKIE

*A Collection of Speeches
and Writings on
Present-Day Issues*

By WENDELL WILLKIE

With a biographical introduction by
STANLEY WALKER

New York
DODD, MEAD & COMPANY

THIS WILL INTEREST ONLY THOSE
WHO THINK OF THE UNITED
STATES AS THEIR LAND—A LAND
THAT THEY KNOW AND LOVE—
A LAND THAT BECAME RICH
THROUGH THE INDUSTRY, THRIFT,
AND ENTERPRISE OF ITS PEOPLE,
AND WILL NEVER REGAIN ITS PROS-
PERITY IN ANY OTHER WAY.

W. L. W.

CONTENTS

This is not an index. The citizen who will vote in November wants to know Mr. Willkie's views on the leading problems of the day. Fortunately, Mr. Willkie has been expressing these views over a period of several years, and a representative collection of his articles and speeches is here presented.

For the convenience of the reader, a subject guide has been compiled so that he may easily satisfy his curiosity about Mr. Willkie's position on important questions. However, these references are by no means complete and the book will richly repay careful reading.

THIS IS WENDELL WILLKIE

A BIOGRAPHICAL INTRODUCTION

By Stanley Walker

THE emergence of Wendell Willkie as a dominant figure on the American political scene has been described
as something of an accident—a happy one, to be sure,
but in the nature of an historical oddity, none the less.

Such an assumption is hardly correct. Willkie is no
Johnny-Come-Lately to the strange science and art of
politics. Politics come as naturally to him as hitting
home runs did to Babe Ruth. His own nature and his
way of life over the years, studying, meeting people,
arguing, listening, disputing, conciliating, would seem
on examination to have pointed him inevitably toward
the place he now occupies.

The seeming miracle at Philadelphia has an unreal
quality simply because the mass of American people,
cynical, though at the same time forever hopeful, are
astonished when a political convention shows ordinary
good sense. There is general wonderment and jubila-
tion when such a conclave, rising above the timidity
which afflicts the ordinary political mind, nominates a
man who is not wholly colorless, evasive in manner, and
smooth as a well-worn pebble. It is odd, but true, that

usually the people hope for a leader with dash and personality while the betting men are inclined to string along with the stuffed shirt.

The actual event, the nomination of Wendell Willkie for President by the Republican Convention, came about through the confluence of forces which, viewed in retrospect, were as nearly irresistible as such things can be. The seers of politics tell us that there are great, mysterious ground-swells of public opinion and feeling which cannot be measured exactly, which cannot always even be explained, but which have about them an inexorable quality.

Willkie, the candidate, is the product of just such powerful and unseen forces. He happened to come along at the right moment, ready-made to fit into his place in the history of our times. As he himself put it two months before his nomination: "I seem to be in front of a trend."

It has been said that Willkie is a "natural." Those who saw him in action in Philadelphia could readily understand what that means. He is his own best salesman, and, as General Hugh S. Johnson once wrote, he generally sells on sight. And he has been at this business of selling himself and his ideas for a long time.

Of all the curiously assorted pro-Willkie forces which converged on Philadelphia (they were a motley army of amateurs, idealists, volunteers and a few seasoned political workers) Wendell Willkie himself was by all odds the most effective. He showed callers something new in candor. He gave straight answers to straight questions. He never dodged a tricky heckler. He pumped the hands of delegates. He spoke to everybody who would listen. He was not above engaging in an impromptu debate in a hotel lobby. His forthrightness was as effective as it was unusual and refreshing.

A novice? In a sense, to be sure, but he knew enough of the ropes to get by. Indeed, by instinct he has always been as good a politician as a business man. When a political boss sent a message to him, suggesting that Willkie enter into an agreement that would have been distasteful and even dangerous to his candidacy, Willkie sent back word: "Tell him no. As we say in Indiana, I didn't drop off the berry bushes yesterday." His frankness appears to be the quality which surprises most observers. And it frightens some. They fear he is too articulate for his own good. But, as one journalist remarked soon after the convention: "That man can make two politically injudicious remarks a day—remarks that would terrify the ordinary politician—and he can still be elected." He has the engaging willingness to say exactly what he thinks, to say it spontaneously, and to say it in words of extraordinary clarity and force.

Willkie's character, as everybody should know by now, is distinctive, but it could hardly be called complex. There are, so far as his oldest friends and associates know, no devious, deep and esoteric currents in his make-up. His traits are plain enough for all to see without benefit of the ministrations of political psychoanalysts. He is, however, the sort of person who is calculated, as if expressly so designed by Nature, to drive even the more cautious and sober word-painters into lyrical passages.

Raymond Moley once pointed out that the "human interest" boys were inclined to hamper Willkie by over-doing his so-called "colorful" characteristics, but that Willkie continued to surge forward because his quali-ties "so far outrun the efforts of his friends to describe them." And then Mr. Moley, succumbing to the very ailment which he had warned against, wrote in the magazine *Newsweek*: "Willkie is as literate as Winston Churchill, as redolent of the American scene as Wil-liam Jennings Bryan and as full of driving energy as Theodore Roosevelt. It is hard to find a parallel to illustrate his qualities as a debater."

This game of "Who is Willkie really like?" has been played by many others besides Mr. Moley. At least one commentator saw in him something of Thomas Jefferson, and certainly he has a good deal of Jeffer-son's simplicity and lack of affectation, coupled with not a little of the hard intellectual fiber of the red-haired Sage of Monticello. Two years ago a young editorial writer with a weakness for coining epithets said, after hearing Willkie make a talk at a luncheon in a club in downtown New York: "There's the Abe Lincoln of Wall Street." And there is something of Lincoln about him. General Johnson, the beloved but occasionally frightening Iron Pants, referred to him in an article in *The Saturday Evening Post* as "a big, tousled bear of a man with a kindly and amused expression." And then the shrewd old General went on with this penetrating passage to describe what many writers have found to be an almost indefinable quality in Willkie:

"It is principally a quality of Will Rogers, who 'never met a man he didn't like.' Mr. Willkie never has to say this. It oozes out of him. He would be as much at ease, maybe more so, in the company of a derelict bum who came to his back door—and many do —as with his college mate, Paul McNutt, and—which is far more important—so would the bum.

"We might call this quality 'charm,' but let's not, because the word for that abstraction has been worn out on Mr. Roosevelt's great and undoubted quality. Franklin could charm a canary out of a tree to sit at a tomcat's supper. The difference is that Mr. Roosevelt has to turn his on for the occasion. Mr. Willkie's seems to be effortlessly working all the time. You can convince yourself of this difference by asking what you would think if Mr. Roosevelt should say, 'I never met a man I didn't like.' He has one of the choicest collections of hates in America. Mr. Willkie has none."

The foregoing probably is a sound enough summing up. But this is not to try to set up Mr. Willkie as a soft and indiscriminate lover of all humanity, washed and unwashed, good and evil. He is nothing of the sort. But he can disagree violently with a man, denounce the man's actions and what he stands for, without stooping to personal vilification. Rancor and meanness and spite and pettiness are not in him. When the smoke has died down he is still in good humor, friendly toward his antagonists. With all this he can be a demon on the attack. And when an opponent in debate begins to back and fill, or fails to hold up his end of the discussion, the disgust on Willkie's face is unmistakable.

To clear up a possible misapprehension: Mr. Willkie is not what is generally known as a wit. But he handles himself in excellent fashion in the give and take of rough and tumble argument, and he has a full enough complement of humor, together with a rare gift for the trenchant phrase. His fund of anecdote and amusing reminiscence is endless and he tells a story well, particularly when the joke is on himself.

Moreover, there seems to be a widespread impression, fostered by well-meaning attempts to "humanize" Mr. Willkie even further than the evidence warrants, that he is a spectacularly sloppy dresser, a long-haired, unkempt fellow who doesn't care whether his clothes are pressed or not. The truth is that although he is no dude, neither is he an uncouth bumpkin in manner or appearance. He orders at least six suits made a year, and they are good suits. Each morning he starts out with a freshly pressed one. He has been known to boast about his taste in picking out a necktie. It is true enough, however, that clothes play a very minor part in his scheme of things, and that he is naturally a pleasantly rumpled sort of fellow. His hair is brown, thick and unruly, and he has a habit of running his hand through it, which adds to the general air of dishevelment. When he has taken some pains for a formal occasion, and is in full evening regalia, with white tie and tails and his hair freshly trimmed, he is a distinguished, even an imposing, figure.

Willkie's unhurried manner, which can be misleading, is in sharp contrast to the crisp, curt demeanor of the traditional big business man. But Willkie apparently never has felt it necessary to conduct himself according to any accepted pattern. Actually he is a tremendous worker, makes quick decisions and can dispose of much detail with speed and sureness of touch. He often has done a day's work before his neighboring tycoons in downtown New York have bestirred themselves sufficiently to get to their offices. One reason is that he seems to need little sleep. He aims at six hours; four or five will do. He wakes early, often plans his day in his mind before he gets out of bed, and has read all the newspapers and had breakfast by eight o'clock. Many a business conference has been conducted across the breakfast table, and his appointments with his dentist are invariably at eight. At the office he goes through work with amazing expedition, finding time in the midst of it to chat with friends (it is always easy to reach him on the phone), to knock off for an occasional baseball game, to inquire into some curious matter quite unrelated to business that may have interested him, and at the end of the day to stop by some friend's house for a visit on the way home. On the other hand, if the occasion demands it, he can be found hard at work in his office all evening.

The "crackerbox" notion about Willkie is not altogether unjustified. His desk at his office is often untidy, littered with books, magazines, documents and letters. At many of the conferences and interviews in his office he puts his feet on the desk. He likes to throw one leg across the arm of a chair when he is engaged in informal discussion. He sprawls. But when the argument gets started, his blue eyes light up, the lines in his face begin crinkling, he starts gesturing with both hands, the slump comes out of his shoulders, and you have Willkie in action. He is six feet one inch tall, weighs around 210 pounds (and doesn't worry about it), and his wide shoulders usually stoop a bit.

Willkie has been described as looking like an Indiana farmer and the description has a certain aptness. All his life he has been interested in growing things. He owns five farms, comprising a total of some 1500 acres, in the neighborhood of Rushville, Indiana. These places are prosperous and well-kept. The families who live on them share the proceeds with him fifty-fifty, and they live well. Willkie himself has made little profit out of this farming venture because he is constantly putting his share of the income back into the farms in the form of improvements. For the most part, the farms are corn and hog enterprises, although he has a few Hereford cattle. Recently he astounded the neighbors by placing general supervision of his land in the hands of a woman, Miss Mary Sleeth, whom he has known for many years and for whose business judgment he has a high regard. He visits the farms as often as he gets the chance, and when he can't visit them he still makes it a point to know what is going on.

He has never owned an automobile, although he likes to be driven through the countryside. When going from his home in upper Fifth Avenue to his office downtown at 20 Pine Street, he would, if in a hurry, take the subway; if he had plenty of time, he would ride down in a taxicab. His favorite taxicab drivers say he is a generous tipper, as well as a friendly, agreeable passenger. He probably would be an unsafe man at the wheel of an automobile. "I am too absentminded to drive," he says. Others say he would not be a good driver because he would be talking and would be sure to make one of his two-handed gestures, letting go of the steering wheel when he should be watching traffic.

He carries no watch. This curious personal quirk has caused much astonishment among those who worry about such foibles. Willkie would be the first to admit that time is fairly important, and that engagements should be kept with reasonable promptness, and that railroads and airplanes have time-schedules to which they must try to adhere, but he has found that fountain pens and watches never stay by him long. So after leaving them in hotel rooms, Pullman berths and washrooms on numerous occasions, he has simply given up carrying them. He will get the time from clocks in windows, or on the street, or he will ask waiters, cab drivers or his secretary. He gets along somehow, and is usually on time.

In his conversation, and particularly if an argument is on foot, Willkie is direct, vigorous and uncommonly alert. He still has more than a trace of his Indiana speech. The word "power," for example (a word which he uses often), he pronounces "par" or "pa'ar." When steamed up, he is something of an exhorter of the old school.

One of Willkie's most useful assets is a genuinely re-markable memory—that, and his ability to draw in-stantly, when the situation arises, upon a vast storehouse of information which he has piled up in his mind. He can lard his discourses with quotations and stories from the Bible, he knows his Shakespeare, he can recite whole passages from the works of James Bryce, and he is an adept at drawing parallels from history.

He is an avid fact-seeker, with a curiosity that would have made him one of the most thorough and versatile newspaper reporters ever heard of. The law and the utility business, which have been his principal outward concerns, are by no means the only fields in which he is an expert—or, if not precisely an expert, at least a man with more than ordinarily detailed knowledge. Facts fascinate him. He can throw out dates and figures in a profusion, and with an exactness that is downright flabbergasting. He doesn't parade this gift unduly, for he is an excellent listener, but it would be difficult to conceive of an argument arising in the normal course of his life in which he could not enter pretty well loaded with information and understanding.

Not only is Willkie a connoisseur of people—all sorts and conditions of people—but he also is a student of towns, why they die, why they grow, why their economic life is out of kilter, and why they have certain social problems. When he goes into a town strange to him, he seeks at once to find out all about that place, to spot its strength and its weakness, to learn what makes its wheels go round. The first three persons he calls upon, not necessarily in the order named, are the town librarian, the leading newspaper editor, and one of the principal bankers. From them he usually can get enough facts and opinion to form an accurate appraisal of what the town is like. And before he leaves, he knows not only how the people are getting along economically but also what they are thinking.

For years, traveling over the vast territory covered by the lines of the Commonwealth & Southern, he has lived a more or less itinerant life, spending as much as 100 days out of the year visiting towns of 2,000 population and more. It was during his visit to one such town that Carl Saunders, editor of the *Citizen Patriot* of Jackson, Michigan, wrote:

"Wendell Willkie has diagnosed wisely a major fault of American big business. The president of the Commonwealth & Southern says that men at the top of a particular business heap become segregated from the public and, as a result, their policies ultimately reflect a lack of understanding of public interest . . . He himself is as approachable as a Pullman porter, as democratic as a candidate for sheriff."

This incessant traveling, although it undoubtedly had its value not only to his business but to the final result of making his personality widely known over a large area, was not undertaken merely as a chore which he thought he should perform. He learned things from it as well, and while he was about it he had a good time. A good time for Willkie means either a chance to talk to somebody or to read. He can enjoy a set-to with a chance acquaintance in a Pullman car and he can have just as much fun passing the time of day with a small-town drug store proprietor.

From boyhood Willkie has had excellent opportunities to study the vagaries, the habits and the aspirations of his fellow-Americans. One summer he drove a bakery wagon; when he was nine he sold newspapers; again he was hired as a barker for a tent hotel during a land boom at Aberdeen, South Dakota; he sweated with threshing crews (the hardest physical labor he ever performed, as he recalls it now) from Oklahoma northward; he was a laborer in California; he moved abandoned town houses out to farms; he worked in a steel mill; he had a job for a time in the sugar lands of Puerto Rico. Those experiences, difficult though some of them were, taught him a great deal about people and about the country, and they also gave him an ease of manner which makes him as much at home sitting on a fence-rail with a farmer as across a table from a Wall Street banker.

Willkie has been charged with being literate and the charge is true. His New York apartment is a virtual granary of books—novels, histories, essays, biographies, everything. And he has read them. He has even written two excellent book reviews for the *New York Herald Tribune's* literary section. Among his particular interests has been the economic history of the South, particularly of Alabama, from its early settlement up to the Civil War. Indeed, he has long thought of writing a book about it, "when I retire." Moreover, he confessed recently:

"I think I could pass a test on English constitutional history with a mark of at least ninety-five."

It is the custom to think of big business men as being not only aggressively non-bookish, but as addicted to sending out dictatorial orders and ukases to department heads. While he was president of Commonwealth & Southern, Willkie sent out only one "general order." That was a note in which he suggested the reading of Margaret Mitchell's novel *Gone with the Wind.* Miss Mitchell's husband was a member of the Georgia Power Company organization, and Willkie thought, as he now tells the story on himself, that he was helping a nice young couple to get started so that they could build the house they had dreamed of.

It is undoubtedly true, as General Johnson was at pains to point out, that the word "charm" has been so overworked that it has lost its flavor (in some quarters it has come to be almost an ugly epithet), but it is by no means the only word that has taken an awful beating. Two others are "liberal" and "democracy," once-useful words which have been mouthed so much, and used for such strange purposes, that they have fallen into an undeserved disrepute. What Willkie means by those words must be fairly clear to any one who has read his speeches or magazine articles; he means them in the old-fashioned, traditional sense, in the way they were used before they had been bandied about by a million parlor dialecticians.

The roots of Wendell Willkie's liberalism and faith in democracy go back a long way. All four of his grandparents came to the United States from Germany in the great political migration of 1848; they, like tens of thousands of others who settled here at that time, were misfits in a country dominated by Prussianism. But they were at home here. There is in all this sturdy, good-living breed an instinctive resentment against autocracy under whatever multifarious names and garments it may show itself. The distinguishing marks of these people (and they may be observed in many parts of America) are a forthright simplicity, a vast capacity for happiness, an uncompromising honesty, a gift for industry—plus an ingrained rebelliousness against any arrogant Big Shot.

The name of the Willkie family was originally Willcke. A strong individualistic strain and a marked ability seem to have run through many members of this family. One of Wendell Willkie's grandmothers was a Presbyterian preacher; an aunt was a doctor. His father, Herman Willkie, and his mother, Henrietta

Trisch, were first school teachers and then lawyers. His mother was the first woman to be admitted to the bar in Indiana.

At the time of the birth of Wendell Willkie, on February 18, 1892, the town of Elwood, Indiana, was flourishing, and Herman Willkie had become a man of considerable substance. Elwood had experienced a tremendous boom. Natural gas had been discovered in large quantities, and this clean and plentiful fuel had attracted many manufacturers, notably makers of tin plate. The city was so prodigal with its gas that the street lights were left on in the daytime; it didn't seem to be worth the trouble to turn them off. The town had forty saloons. It was a bustling place, reeking with frontier juices. Herman Willkie was expanding his real estate holdings, believing in the future of Elwood. The bogs around the town were being drained to make way for some of the richest farm tracts in the country.

Then the bottom fell out. The financial upheaval of 1893 put Herman Willkie through the wringer—along with most of Elwood and many another town. The supply of natural gas failed. Industries shut down or moved away. Parts of Elwood took on the appearance of a ghost city. And its days of glory never came back. The population today is around 10,000; the town gets along, but it no longer dreams of metropolitan greatness.

The family of Herman Willkie (it had been one of leadership, substance and culture in Elwood) had to start again almost from scratch. That is why, in his youth, Wendell Willkie was anything but pampered; the family was not bowed down by poverty, but the sledding was tough. And Herman Willkie was determined that all his children should have an education. For he had the same respect for education that is so marked today in his son. It was a big and lusty family. There were six children: Julia, the oldest, who never married and who is now employed as a bacteriologist in Canada; Robert and Fred, who are officials of Seagram's; next came Wendell; then Edward, a fabulous fellow who is six feet five inches tall, known at Annapolis where he was All-American tackle as Wee Eddie Willkie, and now in charge of salmon canning for Libby's; and last and youngest, Charlotte, the belle of the family, who is married to Commander Paul Pihl, naval attaché at the American Embassy in Berlin.

It was a harum-scarum, disputatious household. The boys in particular were full of high animal spirits. Herman Willkie had a habit of waking his brood by shouting quotations from the classics at them. The dinner table was a place for solid eating; it also resembled a somewhat daffy debating society in full cry. All of Elwood might not admire the Willkies wholeheartedly; one thing was certain—Elwood could not ignore them.

After Elwood's schooling, Wendell Willkie entered the University of Indiana at Bloomington. His two older brothers and his sister Julia, who kept house for them, were in the University at the same time and to-

gether they formed a lively and sometimes rambunc-
tious group. At the same time they were good students.

Chroniclers of Wendell Willkie's college days have
been inclined to overdraw him somewhat and to picture
him as a rebellious, hell-roaring, Socialistic, anti-every-
thing young man. He was hardly as startling as that
description would make him out to be. As to his Socialism, he recalls:

"I had read everything I could get my hands on, including *Das Kapital* by Karl Marx, and I was enormously impressed by it. I wondered why we did not
have a course on Socialism. A faculty member told me
that he would conduct such a course if I could drum
up ten students who were interested. I had to button-
hole almost everyone in the university before I could
get the ten. No wonder they thought of me as a So-
cialist."

After getting his A.B. in 1913, Wendell Willkie
took a position teaching history in the high school at
Coffeyville, Kansas, a place which is principally famous
in history as having been the home of Walter Johnson,
the great baseball pitcher. Willkie was popular at
Coffeyville. He made a good record as a teacher, and
was a competent coach of the track team. After a year
he was offered a raise—from ninety dollars a month to
ninety-five dollars—but he perceived, with no staggering amount of thought on his part, that there was not
much money in that sort of career. He went back to
the university and studied law, getting his degree in

1916, after which he began to practice law with his father.

In the first case that Wendell helped prepare, the Willkie firm won the dissolution of an injunction which had forbidden a labor union to picket. They handled many such cases. Herman Willkie was known as a persistent, and sometimes exasperating, champion of the underdog. With those early days as a background Wendell Willkie says:

"Of course I have no prejudice against the rights of labor. I believe in collective bargaining, and I'm against any business run the paternalistic way, where employees are supposed to be seen and not heard."

Indeed, throughout his later business career, the labor attitude of Wendell Willkie has never been seriously attacked. At least two-thirds of Commonwealth & Southern's operating subsidiaries are unionized. Some have contracts with the C. I. O., some with the American Federation of Labor. There have been few labor troubles.

On the day the United States entered the World War Wendell Willkie enlisted with his brother Robert, a natural enough impulse considering the family's traditional loathing of Prussianism. He soon became a lieutenant in field artillery. He learned to like gunnery, but he could never become over-enthusiastic about rigid army discipline. It was while he was in training at Camp Knox, Kentucky, that he married Miss Edith Wilk, of Rushville, Indiana, who for a time had been secretary of the board of trustees of the library at Elwood. The story has been told a thousand times of how he proposed:

"Edith, how would you like to change that Wilk to Willkie?"

The ceremony was performed, and he went off to the wars. In France, where he became a captain, Willkie got little chance to demonstrate his newly-acquired expertness as an artilleryman. For a time in France, and for some months after he returned to the United States at the close of the war, he was busy defending soldiers who had been court-martialed for infractions of army discipline. In many of these cases Willkie felt that the defendants had been brought up on petty, unjust and sometimes downright nonsensical charges. He won many acquittals. It was excellent experience, sharpening his courtroom technique.

He saw little future in Elwood, and got a job in the legal department of the Firestone Rubber Company at Akron, Ohio. Already he had been asked to run for Congress, but declined—a decision that he never regretted. He worked with Firestone until he was making a salary of $5000 a year, a fair income for that time and place. He yearned, however, for a broader practice, and accepted an offer to join the well-established law firm of Mather and Nesbitt. When old Harvey Firestone heard of his decision he offered to raise him to $10,000 a year, but Willkie had made his choice.

"Young man," said Firestone in parting with him, "I like you, but I don't think you will ever amount to a great deal."

"Why not?" asked Willkie.

"Because," said the rubber magnate, "I understand
you are a Democrat.   No Democrat can ever amount
to much."

This period in Akron with the law firm was probably the making of Wendell Willkie, not only as a professional man but as a public figure.   He worked hard.
He tried many cases.   Sometimes he spent as many
as two hundred days a year in courtrooms.   But that
was not all.   He was not a joiner, but he took part in
discussions of every public issue that came along.   He
espoused the doctrines of Senator Robert Marion La
Follette of Wisconsin (to this day he regards himself
as a good deal of a "La Follette liberal").   He learned
how to get along with newspaper men, no difficult ac-
complishment for a man of his manner and tempera-
ment.   He came out strongly against the Ku-Klux Klan,
denouncing it all over the state, and it must be remembered that this was in a period when many a man "on
his way up in the world" was very cautious about saying anything that might offend the hooded knights.
Having arrived in Akron without a friend or acquaintance, in ten years he had made himself probably the
best trial lawyer in the state and one of the best known
men in northeastern Ohio.   His acquaintance was
enormous, and he achieved it without backslapping,
without joining everything in sight, without playing
golf.

In 1924 Willkie was a delegate to that dreadful,
bitter, long-drawn-out spectacle, the Democratic Na-

tional Convention which ran for three weeks in New
York's old Madison Square Garden. He stood solidly
behind the candidacy of Alfred E. Smith, principally on
the ground that William Gibbs McAdoo was being supported by the Klan and by Klan sympathizers. He had
little more to do with politics until 1932, when he associated himself with a group which sought to bring about
the nomination of Newton D. Baker by the Democrats.

Among the clients of Mather, Nesbitt and Willkie
was the Northern Ohio Power & Light, one of the many
utility properties in which Bernard Capen Cobb of New
York was interested. In 1926 Mr. Cobb, who had been
impressed by Willkie, wrote to an officer of the Ohio
company:

"Do not let this young man get away from us. . . .
He is a comer and we should keep an eye on him."

Meanwhile, Cobb was busy with plans of empire.
He formed the great holding company, Commonwealth
& Southern, with operating units in eleven states from
Michigan to Alabama. In 1929 he brought Wendell
Willkie to New York to join the legal staff of the new
company. Willkie was not particularly enthusiastic
about the idea of living and working in New York, and
he made the move with some misgivings. He reached
the big city in time to see the last months of the fantastic boom era, just before the Great Débâcle came.
It was impressed upon him—something which he already felt was true—that the utility business, in many
of its aspects, could stand reform. One of the questions that often comes up when Willkie is being dis-

cussed is just how much he had to do with Samuel Insull.

He had one contact, and only one, with that gentleman.   That occurred in 1929, when Insull was at the top of his amazing career.   Willkie attended a meeting of utility men at which Insull was complaining against radicals, "loose talk," and the critics of Big Business, who, he felt, should be silenced in some fashion.   Such an opinion was diametrically opposed to everything that Willkie had ever believed or felt. When called upon for his opinion, he argued for the free and untrammeled expression of criticism, no matter from what source.   It would, he contended, be good both for the country and for business.   When Willkie had finished, Insull turned to him and said:

"Mr. Willkie, when you are older, you will know more."

When Mr. Cobb retired in 1933 as head of Commonwealth & Southern, there was no question about the man who would succeed him.   Willkie naturally moved into the job.   He took the title of president, but declined that of chairman of the board because it somehow sounded too pompous—and besides, he held the title was unnecessary.   One of his first acts was to revamp the membership of his board of directors.   He managed to remove most of the bankers.   Then he set about to build up the business.   He did not have to introduce any drastic reforms, because, as *Fortune* magazine diagnosed the situation, "there wasn't a hell of a lot to reform."

Willkie made $75,000 a year as president of Com-

monwealth & Southern.   Once, when it became known
that he had declined an increase in salary, he was reported to have said that he did not think any one should
receive more than the President of the United States.
A neat remark, and one that received much publicity,
but not strictly accurate. His real attitude was:

"Naturally I like to make money. But as head of
a company that has been through hard times, and which
has been trying to get back on its feet, along with the
rest of industry, I doubted the propriety of taking more
money. It would be out of line."

He has since declined at least two jobs which would
have paid him $250,000 a year, not because he was
averse to taking the money, but because he did not want
to abandon the fight he had been making on behalf of
Commonwealth & Southern. And when he finally resigned, following his nomination as Presidential Candidate, he declined "severance pay" of $75,000. He
simply didn't feel it belonged to him. However, if
anyone has the idea that Mr. Willkie has an anchorite's
contempt for money, a grave mistake is being made.
He likes to earn the stuff and he likes to spend it,
though his ways of spending it are not the orthodox
ways of pleasure. His personal expenditures are small
and his personal habits simple. But a close friend admits that he "must have sent at least fifty boys and girls
through college."

When Willkie became head of his big company the
income of utilities had gone down and down until the
situation was almost hopelessly bleak. The brains of

the business expected even worse days to come. Sales were off. People were not buying refrigerators, washing machines, or anything else that they could avoid. Companies were trying to cut expenses by laying off salesmen. The utility business was at its lowest ebb in public estimation. It had a consistently "bad press." The memory of Insull, which could hardly be dismissed lightly, persisted everywhere.

One of the first moves Willkie made was to hire five hundred new salesmen and launch a campaign, a tremendous go-getting crusade, to sell more electrical appliances. He liberalized the terms of credit. In order to stimulate the use of power in private houses, he put forward a new scheme, known now in the business as "the objective rate." This is a system under which a householder receives a bonus in the form of free electricity; but, of course, to get this bonus, he must use electricity liberally. Thus, if a consumer will use $3.50 worth of electricity a month, an extra one-third of that amount can be had for nothing.

This move on Willkie's part—and it was an extraordinarily bold one—was successful. It was a tremendous gamble, fool-proof in theory but opposed to the practical judgment of many of Willkie's colleagues. In six years the amount of electricity sold by the Commonwealth & Southern companies more than doubled; the sale of domestic equipment by his companies rose from less than $5,000,000 to more than $20,000,000 a year; this business was also good for independent dealers in equipment who covered the same territory. *And the*

rates came down. Today they are about thirty per cent
less in the Commonwealth & Southern system than the
average for the rest of the country. The theory back
of Willkie's daring move has been most succinctly
summed up by General Johnson:

"He had a scheme to get rates down and electrical
consumption up—on the principle that the only way to
get prices down is to get consumption up. That is also
the theory of the Government's TVA and REA and
Henry Ford and of American mass production in
general. It proves on paper. The sticking point in
practice is 'which must come first—the increased consumption or the lower price?' It takes a lot of nerve to
cut prices far below cost at existing sales volumes, on the
gamble that the increased business will come to save
you. It takes nerve and a period of time—sometimes
so long that the gambler busts his company and ruins
his stockholders before the principle can prove."

The problem in front of Willkie was to achieve his
purpose, getting prices down and consumption up, without taking too big a gamble with his stockholders. And
the one way to do this was through salesmanship. Willkie himself became a salesman. He had no press to
help him (no "kept press" as the fine old phrase has it)
in any of the eleven states where he operated. He had
no need of such a thing. He wandered over the country like a super-peddler, talking his wares. He has
often described himself as "the best gadget salesman
in the country." He tried to prove that utilities were
not necessarily inventions of the devil. He argued

that there was no real reason why a utility should be in constant dispute with its customers. He was enormously persuasive. Rate fights, which can be ruinously costly, were stopped wherever possible. And while this was going on, and Mr. Willkie was looming larger and larger as the most articulate force in Big Business, something else was happening without his quite realizing it: He was selling Wendell Willkie to the people.

It was, however, Willkie's titanic joust with the New Deal over the Tennessee Valley Authority's policies that brought him his greatest public notice. In this fight he both lost and won. Probably his chief gain, outside of protecting his stockholders, was in the public realization that here was a man who could hold his own when pitted against some of the trickiest minds of the New Deal. Most big business men are not at their best when sitting in a witness chair. They can read a statement, and then they sit there and get torn to bits. Willkie not only could protect himself; he knew how to take the offensive.

The story of the fight really goes back to 1933, when David Lilienthal, a former member of the Wisconsin Utility Commission and a foe of private ownership from way back, became a member of the TVA. It was in the cards from the beginning that Lilienthal intended to chase every private utility out of the Tennessee Valley region. Lilienthal became chairman of TVA in 1937 after the dismissal, amid acrimony, of Arthur E. Morgan, a former president of Antioch College.

At the beginning of the TVA project, Willkie was able to reach an agreement by which Commonwealth & Southern exchanged power with TVA and was free of government competition in certain areas. This agreement expired in 1937, and meanwhile TVA had spread over the whole valley. And it was part of the scheme to encourage towns to build or buy city-owned distributing plants with government money. The TVA lines spread out beside private lines, with cheap power which was, in part at least, made possible because TVA paid no taxes and operated under a curiously elastic capital structure—a circumstance which caused Willkie to remark that, with TVA's privileges, he could sell power thirty-five per cent cheaper than TVA was selling it.

Strangled and surrounded by such competition, the utilities were isolated, cut off from new capital markets. Willkie suggested private operation under government supervision; he advocated a revolving fund of $100,-000,000 to finance private rural expansion, meanwhile promising low rates if large-scale operation could be brought about. To all of this he met rebuffs. He offered to sell his valley properties at "any reasonable figure," and this offer also was refused. Testifying before a Congressional committee which was investigating the working of TVA, he offered to sell at a price to be fixed by the Securities Exchange Commission. This suggestion also was turned down. Then, when the situation seemed deadlocked, negotiations were resumed.

The upshot of further conferences was that Commonwealth & Southern sold its operating subsidiary, the Tennessee Electric Power Company, for $78,600,-000. This agreement was completed in July, 1939. The amount agreed upon, according to Willkie, was less than the worth of the properties, but it was considerably more than the first suggestions made by the government. Willkie's tactics in getting up the price have been described as his "$30,000,000 shriek."

Willkie's conduct of this fight won him the respect, and in many instances the friendship, of some of the leading lights of the New Deal, including Lilienthal himself. Indeed, Lilienthal called Willkie one of the outstanding proponents of private enterprise "who has done a real job of selling electricity at low rates." In a sense, however, Willkie took a beating, because he lost his properties in the valley. But it is largely because of Willkie's fight to present his case to the public that Congress is now highly critical of TVA and all similar projects, and that the word "yardstick" is seldom heard these days.

Convinced that in a democracy one should take one's case to the people, Mr. Willkie has been explicit in setting forth his views on a large number of public questions. He has attracted attention by the felicity and directness of his sentences. Speaking up and down the country, and writing occasional magazine articles, he has spread his opinions over a wide area, so that there can be no mistake about his beliefs. To some observers one of the most startling facts about his credo is that he makes no defense for the evils and excesses of Big

Business, particularly during the boom years. He says that "the magic touch of power" was a corrupting influence in those years. But he adds:

"Power is just as destructive on Pennsylvania Avenue as it was in Wall Street. Power goes to men's heads. When you see the bust of Napoleon on the desk of a business man, you'd better get out quick and sell him short. The same goes for government officials."

Although he has been one of the most eloquent voices in the defense of private ownership, and believes that business should be allowed to make a fair profit on invested capital, he is in favor of regulation of abuses. He even admits that stringent government regulation of utilities has in some instances caused companies to improve their methods to the great benefit of all concerned. Moreover, he holds that private utilities have no "God-given charter" for existing, and that there is no reason why the government should not put them out of business if the people want the government to do so. He has, however, quoted many times the statement of Thomas A. Edison, which he believes sums up perfectly the defects of government ownership:

"There is far more danger in public monopoly than there is in private monopoly, for when the government goes into business, it can pretend to sell cheap power and then cover up its losses. The government never really goes into business, for it never makes ends meet, and that is the first requisite of business. It just mixes a little business with a lot of politics, and no one ever gets a chance to find out what is actually going on."

Mr. Willkie has often argued for the view that private industry can promote recovery by lowering prices and increasing consumption, with the corollaries of greater production and increased employment. He holds that the government falls into a patent absurdity when it says that it "spreads benefits" by limiting enterprise and production and confiscating the property of one class for the benefit of another. This, he contends, is simply destructive, a spreading of scarcity and, in its final effects, poverty. Above all, he objects to the scrambling of our theories of government—the theory that we can be part paternalistic, part totalitarian, and still be part democratic. What has happened in the United States in the last eight years, he contends, is the growth of a dangerous threat which he calls Big Government.

In 1932 he approved so thoroughly of the Democratic platform that he voted for Franklin D. Roosevelt, contributing $150 to the campaign. He has said since that he wished he had the money back. He still approves of the 1932 platform, however. "I did not leave the Democratic Party," he says. "The party left me." Although he has made furious and sweeping attacks upon virtually the whole broad front of New Deal domestic policy and theory, he has never hesitated to approve, in essence, of many of its aims. But any detailed summary of his position on various questions is unnecessary here; he does that job much better for himself.

Willkie's public reputation as a speaker probably dates from his famous debate with Robert H. Jackson at Town Hall, New York, in January, 1938. Jackson is a talented adversary in any forensic encounter. He is a shrewd lawyer from up-State New York and one of Roosevelt's favorites. Every now and then, before the debate, a trial balloon would go up suggesting that Jackson would make a splendid candidate for Governor of New York—with the Presidency somewhere in the offing. All Jackson booms died that night, although Jackson, in the opinion of many in the audience, held up his end adequately. General Johnson, however, reported that Willkie had made "a perfect monkey" of Jackson; Raymond Moley said that although Jackson's set speech went off in good shape, "Willkie so utterly outclassed him that the Jackson build-up dissolved into the elements from which it came."

That encounter not only went over a national radio hook-up but was widely reported in the newspapers. Willkie also handled himself well at the *New York Herald Tribune* Forum in 1938, when he replied to speeches by W. O. Douglas, then chairman of the Securities Exchange Commission, and Thurman Arnold, Assistant Attorney General. More and more he came to be in demand as a speaker.

Long ago certain individuals were saying privately that Wendell Willkie was Presidential timber, although the idea was usually dismissed as being obviously ridiculous because of the incubus of Big Business, particularly the utility curse. As early as May, 1937, *Fortune* published an article on him and his company. But it was Alva Johnston's *Saturday Evening Post* article, "The Man Who Talked Back" in February, 1939, that first really caught the public attention. During that year some of the talk began to get into newspaper columns. The ball was rolling, but slowly. Last winter General Johnson, in an offhand reply to a question asked after he had made a speech in New York, offered the opinion that if Willkie were nominated, he would make a powerful candidate and, if elected, a great President. This remark got wide publicity, and Willkie, confronted with Johnson's statement by a reporter in Atlanta, said:

"If the government keeps on taking my business away at its recent rate, I'll soon be out of work and looking for a job. Johnson's offer is the best I've had yet."

The "We Want Willkie" talk began to look a shade more serious, but the thought of nominating him was still one of those things that, while they sound good, must be dismissed as naïve by all practical men.

The next step in the steady progress of the Willkie movement came when the April, 1940, issue of *Fortune* appeared with an unusually powerful article by Willkie, entitled "We, the People." It was the most cogent, the most moving, and the most comprehensive statement of his beliefs that he had ever made. Its impact in many quarters was so hard that the Willkie stock

moved up many pegs. Even his son Philip, then advertising manager of the *Daily Princetonian,* remarked
that he had discovered recently that "when I say my
name is Willkie, it means something to people."

Then came, wholly unexpectedly, a young flaming
apostle who had never even met Mr. Willkie. This
man, Oren Root, Jr., a serious-minded lawyer of
twenty-nine, with no experience in politics, began running small advertisements boosting Willkie and distributing petitions urging his nomination by the Republican Convention. Things were moving faster now.
The invitations to speak piled up high on Willkie's desk
on the twenty-first floor of 20 Pine Street—"a block,"
as he used to say, "away from Wall Street."

One day the newspapers carried the announcement
that Russell Davenport had resigned as Managing Editor of *Fortune* in order to devote all his time to helping put Willkie in the White House. Willkie was genuinely alarmed by Davenport's decision, and begged
him not to throw up his job for a cause that had such
a remote chance of success. But Davenport, a novice
at politics, insisted that he knew what he was doing,
and immediately started organizing. Willkie, somewhat reluctantly, gave him his blessing.

By this time press comment was mounting, and
Willkie was astonished and delighted at the common
refrain which ran through all this—that if the Republicans knew what was good for them they would nomi-
nate him. Now, it might be borne in mind that Willkie
never said he didn't want to be President; he was guilt-

less from the beginning of any such coyness. His position merely was that he didn't think he had a chance
for the nomination and that he was not seeking it.
Then other things happened. The Gallup poll showed
him steadily moving up in popularity. Willkie agreed
one night to appear on the radio program "Information, Please," along with those prodigious savants,
Franklin P. Adams, Oscar Levant and John Kieran.
He was gambling more heavily, perhaps, than he realized that night, for of all the spots in the United States
at the present time in which a man can make a complete
ass of himself—and before a nation-wide audience—
this "Information, Please" program is it. But he came
through well, answering difficult questions easily and
promptly. And his easy, friendly personality carried
over the air.

It was not until the middle of May that Willkie himself began to feel that he had something more than
a glimmering of a chance. Soon he was in the fight to
win. By the time he went to Philadelphia he was flatly
predicting that he would get the nomination—"on the
fifth or sixth ballot," he said. He had noise with him,
and plenty of publicity, for people all over the country
bombarded the delegates with demands for his nomination. Professional politicians said that he could
never get started. But Willkie knew something. He
knew that among some of the leaders, and among a
great many of the rank and file of the delegates, there
were many who viewed him favorably and would support him as soon as they saw their chance.

What happened at Philadelphia has been discussed and dissected by dozens of experts, and is ancient history now. Willkie directed his forces like a seasoned general, unconventional though some of his moves may have appeared at the time. He was fortunate in his managers on the floor, notably Governor Harold E. Stassen of Minnesota. He showed good judgment in not seeking aid from certain old-line bosses. It was not merely intuitive good manners, but incidentally excellent political savvy, which caused him to refrain from saying a word against any of his opponents. He was selling Willkie, not running down any one else. Rumpled, sleepless, good-natured, always alert, smoking one cigarette after another, he saw the thing through to the sixth ballot victory. The galleries became the voice of the people shouting, "We Want Willkie." It was the triumph of a ground-swell—that "trend" that Willkie had thought he observed some time earlier—over smoothly greased machine politics.

When some one does a favor for Willkie (and he is the sort of person whom many men and women appear eager to please), he has an old-fashioned phrase which he uses to express his surprise and pleasure.

"Why," he will say, with just a trace of shyness, "I'm touched." Never any long speech—just "I'm touched." At the end of the Philadelphia Convention he was "touched."

It is probable that few other candidates for President ever looked forward to a campaign with more eagerness than Willkie looks forward to this "campaign of ideas." He has had plenty of excellent forums on which to get his doctrines across, but never one like this. And he really wants to be President. No dragooning has been necessary here. He enjoys the hustings as Dempsey used to enjoy swinging his iron fists.

The many facets of this man's personality, most of them curiously engaging, will come out inevitably in the campaign. Most of them are already pretty well on the record. But there is one trait which must be emphasized again because it is so unusual that it borders on the unbelievable: that is, his lack of venom. Most men in public life manage, not always by preference, to pile up a fairly long aggregation of bitter personal enemies. It's hard for an active, outspoken man to avoid feuds which leave scars. And public life ordinarily is conducted in an atmosphere which has more than a trace of suspicion, hatred and worse. Nevertheless, it seems to be true that Willkie, the big fellow who can shout defiance at his opponents in the realm of ideas, has managed to avoid any suggestion of either vituperation or ordinary petulance.

He is what is known around places where men gather as "a stand-up fighter." Not even the cute beagles of the New Deal have been able to get anything "on" him. His business and professional record has already stood the closest scrutiny. His frankness is completely disarming. He is simply a big two-fisted Middle Western American who happens, by one of those inexplicable freaks of fate, to be at the same time a scholar and a gentleman. He is his own walking Brain Trust, and writes all of his own speeches. And, in any gathering, he is about as anonymous and inconspicuous as a buffalo bull in a herd of range cattle.

THE FAITH THAT IS
AMERICA

THE FAITH THAT IS AMERICA

Reprinted from
THE READER'S DIGEST,
December, 1939.

THE FAITH THAT IS
AMERICA

By *Wendell Willkie*

EVER since its founding, the United States has had a special reputation among all nations—a reputation which led millions of people to come to it, and many millions more, who could not migrate, to regard it as the land of heart's desire. This reputation is founded upon one simple fact: in the United States the plain man has always had a chance.

For centuries the ancestors of both my father and my mother lived in Central Europe. Some of them were peasants, some were engaged in semi-professional work, some were artisans, others were landed proprietors; but all of them, through those centuries, had been restricted in their opportunities to the group in which they were born, and no one of them had ever known the true meaning of liberty.

Those people who did not observe the restrictions under which they were forced to live, got into trouble: one had to flee his native land because he adopted the religion of his choice; another was ostracized because he believed in the principles of the French Revolution; and still another was jailed for his insistence on his right to express his own opinions. Until at last, in 1848, my father and my grandparents came to America to escape this absolutism in government and repression of individual liberties.

My father and mother were of the first generation in both families to grow up in America. My mother became a lawyer, the first woman to be admitted to the Indiana bar. My father was also a lawyer, and after marriage my parents practiced law together. Of course, in the Europe from which they came, my mother would have found it impossible to practice a profession; and my father would have found it extremely difficult to get out of the groove worn by his ancestors. Furthermore, it would have been utterly impossible for them to give their six children the education which they received in America. But because of our free educational system, they were able to send their children to school, high school, and college.

And with schooling finished, there were no doors closed to those children just because they came from a plain family in a small town. No one asked them about their social background; no class distinction and no law interfered with their desire to earn a living in the occupation of their choice, or to express their opinions as they pleased. In all the long history of their family, those six children were the first to know, from the time they were born, the blessings of freedom. I don't want them to be the last.

I use my own family as an illustration only because I know about it best. Its record, however, is the record

of any number of American families today. Thus, for
me, as for many other Americans, the value of freedom
has had a practical demonstration. Freedom means for
us not only a theoretical ideal, but definite practical
rights.

Freedom means that if you run a store, you can sell
your products to anybody without a government official
telling you what the prices must be. It means that, if
you are a professor in a university, you don't have to
alter science or delete history as a bureaucrat pre-
scribes. If you own a newspaper, you don't limit your
editorial opinions to what an official censor approves.
If you are a laborer, you can leave your job when you
feel so inclined for any other job you prefer; you can
join a union or not, as you please; you can bargain collectively with your fellow-workers on the conditions of
your work. If you think that taxes are too high, you
can vote against those officials you think responsible.
And there is no limitation upon your inherent American
right to criticize anybody, anywhere, at any time.

These instances are taken at random to indicate the
practical application of this thing called freedom. In
this country we take it for granted—perhaps too much
for granted. But in more than half the world freedom
does not exist. The present conflict in Europe is peril-
ous to this freedom because in a modern war people
destroy the very things they say they are fighting for.
It is because we wish to preserve our free democratic
system that we must remain at peace. But we cannot
remain *carelessly* at peace. If the price of democracy

in ordinary times is eternal vigilance, in a war-period that vigilance must be doubled.

We must be careful that, under the guise of "emergency," the powers of government are not so extended as to impair the vitality of free enterprise and choke off free expression of thought. Those who want the government to run America and make up the minds of the American people are already taking advantage of the growing war psychology.* Already we hear of the need for the government to control prices, to license American business, to regiment American employees and employers, to censor the radio.

In a critical time there is always a temptation to surrender the responsibilities of a free citizen, to say to the government: "During this emergency, you take charge. You tell us what to do, what to think. You fix prices and production, control the press and the radio." But if we should yield to this temptation, the end of our free democratic system might come as readily in peace as in war. Once these responsibilities of citizenship are given up, they are not readily returned. Government, after all, in its practical working consists only of aggregations of men; and men, having tasted power or having found a means by which to put their social theories into effect, do not easily surrender power. We must not be misled because suggested restrictions are for humanitarian purposes, for, as ex-Justice Louis D. Brandeis recently said: "Experience should teach us to be most on our guard to protect liberty

* Written in December, 1939.

when the government's purposes are beneficent. . . . The greatest dangers to liberty lurk in insidious encroachment by men of zeal, well-meaning but without understanding."

The war has not changed the grave domestic questions confronting America; it has just temporarily diverted our minds from them. For ten years we have been haunted by our unemployment problem. We have tried a number of different experiments to solve it, without success. And yet the solution has been in our hands for some time. During the depression decade, for example, American industry accumulated an enormous deficiency in plants and modern machinery. To supply this deficiency industry will need even more than the present number of unemployed. Industry will also need a great deal of additional capital, and there should be no difficulty in getting this, as soon as the millions of American investors are reassured as to the future of free private enterprise.

Such assurance, however, is now lacking. The Secretary of the Treasury spoke some time ago of the "what's-the-use?" attitude of businessmen—small businessmen as well as big. You have seen it yourself: people who say, "What's the use in making a profit? The government will take it all." Workers who say, "Why get a job? I can get nearly as much on relief." Manufacturers who say, "Why take the risk in building a plant? The situation is too uncertain."

And there is also a lack of confidence within industry itself. This is partly a result of industry's own defects and abuses in the period of speculation and over-expansion which ended in 1929. Since that time we have had several years of reform; but some of these reforms have gone so far as to impair both the efficiency and the morale of all American business. In promoting recovery, the chief emphasis has been placed upon what the *government* should do; we have had colossal expenditures for "priming the pump," and a colossal tax program to pay for these expenditures. Here is just the point where our free democracy is threatened. We are not in immediate danger of losing our freedom of speech, or of press, or of worship. The greatest threat to the American system today comes from the effort to restrict free competitive enterprise. And such enterprise alone can make economic recovery possible.

We have been told that the frontiers are gone, that the established American industries are slowing down, and that there is little to be expected in the way of new inventions. We have even been informed that the very basis of the American dream is no longer true; that there isn't much future for the young man in America; that, in short, the plain man no longer has much of a chance. But this defeatist attitude is distinctly alien to America. Let us get rid of it! For such a philosophy is as false as it is cowardly. It is true that we no longer have new geographical frontiers; but other frontiers remain for searching and adventurous minds. Our people, though they are only seven per cent of the world's population, still control more than forty-five per cent of the world's wealth. And we enjoy the highest real wages, the shortest working hours, and the greatest percentage of home ownership on earth.

The great days of America are by no means done. We have only touched the border of our achievement. If I did not believe this, I would not believe in America. Because that faith *is* America.

So my creed, if I were asked to define it, would run something like this:

I believe in America because in it we are free—free to choose our government, to speak our minds, to observe our different religions;

—Because we are generous with our freedom—we share our rights with those who disagree with us;

—Because we hate no people and covet no people's land;

—Because we are blessed with a natural and varied abundance;

—Because we set no limit to a man's achievement—in mine, factory, field, in business or the arts, an able man, regardless of class or creed, can realize his ambition;

—Because we have great dreams—and because we have the opportunity to make those dreams come true.

HOW CAN GOVERNMENT AND BUSINESS WORK TOGETHER?

HOW CAN GOVERNMENT AND BUSINESS WORK TOGETHER?

A DEBATE

BY THE HONORABLE ROBERT H. JACKSON
AND MR. WENDELL WILLKIE

This address was delivered by Mr. Willkie on America's Town Meeting of the Air, broadcast over the Blue Network of the National Broadcasting Company on January 6, 1938, and is here reprinted from TOWN MEETING, BULLETIN OF AMERICA'S TOWN MEETING OF THE AIR, published by Columbia University Press. The other speaker on the broadcast was Robert H. Jackson, then Assistant Attorney General of the United States.

HOW CAN GOVERNMENT AND BUSINESS WORK TOGETHER?

CHAIRMAN DENNY: *Tonight we bring you a program that is a typical example of the kind of thing "America's Town Meeting of the Air" was founded to present. This is not a debate. It is not our purpose to widen cleavages but rather to find common ground upon which all classes and all groups of American citizens may work toward our general welfare. How can government and business work together? That is our subject. I know of none more interesting or important for this nation. We have been extremely fortunate in securing as our speakers the Hon. Robert H. Jackson, Assistant Attorney General of the United States, and Mr. Wendell L. Willkie, President of the Commonwealth and Southern Corporation. At the close of their addresses we will have the usual question period from the audience. It is now my very great pleasure to introduce our first speaker, Mr. Robert H. Jackson, Assistant Attorney General of the United States.*

MR. JACKSON: Probably no two men, who personally respect each other enough to appear in public together, could look at the relations of government to business through more differently colored glasses than Mr. Willkie and myself. I have admired his consistent willingness to stand up man-fashion and submit his views to the test of dispassionate but frank discussion. This is the only process by which a democratic people can reach decisions on conflicting policies. I have recently paid my respects to that small but loud section of business which has been "ganging up" on democracy. So tonight I can address myself to that larger number who submit their case to the sound judgment of democracy.

Business means one thing to Mr. Willkie and another to me. In professional life I was a lawyer chiefly for what we would call small business. My stake in that is far more permanent and important to me than any stake in politics. And in government my particular job is to try to use the archaic anti-trust laws to preserve this same kind of small and independent business. Mr. Willkie, on the other hand, has become not only one of the outstanding lawyers for big business, but his mastery of finance and administration has carried him to the presidency of one of the largest public utility holding corporations in the nation.

Small business of course has its problems with government, one of the chief of which is the correction of inequities in the tax structure. But it is chiefly big business that is at war on many fronts with government. The most constructive thing we can do tonight is to analyze the reasons why they do not get along.

First of all, there is one thing which the people expect business as a whole somehow to do. That is, to furnish steady jobs for all who want to work and to furnish enough goods to make up that standard of living which we have come to regard as American. The public is convinced that a proper economic arrangement, in a nation of such unlimited resources, can give that, and so am I. First we look to business for it. But, if industry will not provide it, the people are determined to provide it for themselves through their government. This nation has repudiated for all time what Senator Wagner has so well called "the outmoded dogma that the helpless must help themselves." A man off the payroll is a man on the tax roll. And whether or not business likes this as a philosophy, it must face it as a fact.

There are those who answer that private enterprise can take care of itself—that all government needs do is "let business alone." Let's see about that. It is important, if true—and it isn't true.

This circle of American private enterprise has never been continuously self-sustaining. It has always operated under concealed subsidies. Until the end of the last century we operated a WPA by which the unemployed could get a quarter section of public land just for occupying it. Then came the second WPA—government borrowing and spending for the World War. After the war came the third WPA. We went into a foreign boon-doggling program. American investors furnished funds—which they lost—which ran a WPA, building schools and highways and housing in Europe and South America.

We no longer have these costly but concealed subsidies to take up the slack in employment. Private enterprise in America today is in a situation where chiefly its own workers are its customers, and its customers are its own workers. Unless it can keep the circle of goods and wages moving, then the government directly and brazenly must fill the gap in employment on one hand, and the needs for goods on the other. We are right out in the open with sheer naked taxes on private enterprise for cash relief. That system can grow to Heaven knows what!

Government last year tried to coöperate with the business demand to get out of government spending, and the problem has come back with increased intensity. What then can we do?

There is, to my mind, an essential first step. That is for big business deliberately and speedily to go to a policy of high volume production, low price, and the highest wage scale possible. As one industry has put the philosophy, we must have more goods for more people at less cost. Steel prices can not be geared to produce profits at 45 per cent of capacity. Building materials must be priced so that building may go on from year to year, as needed. Building industries can not prosper if we can afford to build only in the years when we can afford to be extravagant.

In business that is really competitive, prices adjust themselves. But today a few companies in each industry have grown so powerful that they can, by various devices not reached by present laws, hold prices up for a long time even if they lose customers. They have a short-sighted philosophy that it is better policy in the long run to sell less goods at high prices than more goods at lower prices. Steel has declined in production from nearly 90 per cent of capacity to nearly 30 per cent without dropping the price a cent. It is interesting to know that even the government cannot get really competitive bids for steel. For example, bids for reinforcement bars for Fort Peck dam were filed by ten companies, but each bid was exactly $253,633.80 —identical to a penny. That could not happen in a truly competitive industry. Indeed, there are reputable economists who believe it would not happen even in a wisely managed monopoly.

Steel is not alone in this policy. Important basic industries, notably those supplying building materials, have followed the same policy and have simply priced us out of a housing program.

The other day when General Motors laid off 30,000 men Mr. Knudsen, their President, stated as one of the reasons, "I think the price level rose too fast in the spring of 1937, and we just could not get adjusted to it."

This dramatizes the fact that there is a silent economic conflict in this country between two kinds of industry. On the one hand we have high price, low volume industries, largely in the monopoly or semi-monopoly class. On the other hand we have competitive industry, large and small. Competitive industry is much dependent on non-competitive industry for its raw materials. The automobile industry as a whole has been competitive and has followed a high volume, low price policy. The unprecedented growth of this industry has been due to the fact that it did not shut down its plant and wait for the people to get rich enough to buy cars. It tried to make cars that people could buy without waiting to become rich.

I hope to see anti-monopoly laws enacted that will be adequate to throw the power of organized government back of those businesses which are pursuing a policy of serving the public with an abundance of goods at prices it can afford to pay.

This brings us to another problem that faces both business and the government. Mr. Knudsen gave another and very illuminating reason for laying off those 30,000 men. One reason was, he said, that new cars could not be sold, and the reason for that was that used cars could not be sold. In other words, one reason why those men are out of work tonight is that there is not enough buying power in the particular kind of people who certainly would buy used cars if they could.

But it has been the underlying policy of this New Deal Administration to raise the incomes of just this sort of people. The Administration has tried to keep the used car market open. On June 2, 1937, I opened the Congressional hearings on behalf of the President's proposal for a minimum wage bill to put a floor under depressed wages and to keep up purchasing power. The Wagner Labor Relations Act, to give labor the right to bargain collectively so that it could intelligently and effectively protect its own purchasing power, was an Administration measure. Farm bills and relief measures have been advanced with the very purpose of helping purchasing power—purchasing power of this very low income group who are the people who are willing to take on the used car.

I do not need to point out the opposition; it announces itself. Big business opposition, in my opinion, has been as short-sighted as suicide. A low-wage policy is inconsistent with the standard of living which American business is organized to serve. Unless it is willing to pay wages which will sustain a high standard of American living, it cannot have a market for the commodities which only a high standard of living will call for.

From all these important things the people want business to do, I now turn to an all-important thing they want business not to do.

They do not want all of the business of the country to be swallowed up by a few corporations. So long as the American spirit lives, and democracy survives, so that its spirit can be expressed in law, the American Congress will be trying to break down the concentration of power just as fast as the imperialists of business pile it up. We are a proud people raised on the doctrines of equality found in the Declaration of Independence. We do not like to be bossed too much, not even by a boss whom we know we can change through the ballot box. We do not like to have any one man or corporation own the town.

Because we are a democratic people we are a friendly and sociable people. We know the corner grocer, the automobile dealer, the fellow who runs the factory and the men who run the bank. We know that they are harassed by the pressures of bigger competitors, and by the prices of big industries that control their supplies. We do not care if, and we do not believe it is true that, the big concerns that swallow up these local business men do any better job, on the whole, for our community.

This fear of concentration represented by an anti-big-business feeling is one of the strongest instincts in American politics. Through the centuries people have been afraid of anyone's getting control of too much land, the basic resource of an agricultural civilization. The same instinct bids us now to keep power companies from getting too much of the nation's electric energy, because this is a basic resource of the coming industrial civilization.

This is the point where Mr. Willkie has his difficulties with the government. Mr. Willkie is a good operator—especially with the TVA alongside of him to strengthen his resolve to be good. But Mr. Willkie represents control of utility systems in six states through one great holding company. It is the democratic instinct of our people that arises in the holding company law. People would feel more comfortable if Mr. Willkie could control only two or three states. That simple illustration is typical of many of the contests between concentrated controls of business and popular government.

We have no present substitute for a system of private enterprise motivated by private profit, whatever its defects. To my practical mind, our job is to make the system that is here work. It will take all the strength and intelligence of both business and government to make it work under existing foreign and domestic stresses.

But the business man asks, "Are there not risks in departing from old policies?" Yes, risk is the condition of winning, and consider the risks you take in not changing. Count the cost of not doing it against the cost of doing it. Business needs protection from stagnation far more than from adventure. Remember, the tax collector has to be most busy when industry is idle, in order to complete the circle with tax funds. We must reform to conserve.

Mr. Willkie was one of the pioneers—stimulated no doubt by a little competition from TVA—in the adoption of a low price, high volume basis for his industry. He ventured and it paid.

Business should get over thinking about men in public life as being different from themselves. There are dumb plays in government, matched by some in business. There is waste and incompetence in government, but get any banker's opinion, privately expressed, of some of his debtors' operations. I have seen politics interfere with administrative efficiency in government. I have also seen personal and family and banker politics do some pretty weird things in business. I have charged off enough small investments so that I am not sure big business men are any more infallible than politicians. In fact, I don't know which brand of wisdom I distrust the most, that of the theorists who have studied a business but never run one, or that of the executives who have run a business but never studied it.

The greatest difference between the man I meet in government and the man I meet in business is this: The man who is in government is brought in contact with the problems of all kinds and conditions of men. Everybody's business is his business. He looks at society, if he does his duty, as a whole mechanism rather than specializing his interest in a single business. The private business man, on the other hand, up to now has been intensely preoccupied with a very narrow sector of the world. He has seldom looked about to see the effect which his acts may be having upon the lives of other people. It is this fundamental difference in viewpoint that occasions much of the conflict between business and government.

The difficulty in getting along with business is not so much that it has a bad philosophy of the functions of government as that it has no philosophy as to the broader functions of itself. It tends to make great strife over temporary irritations and it passes unnoticed fundamental menaces to its long-range interest.

Our need now is to settle upon a common objective for business and government. My little contribution is to suggest this program of high volume, low price industrial economy, which will sustain a high wage scale, which in turn will support a high standard of living, which will demand and pay for the high volume production, at prices determined by its wages. The economic organization must find ways in its bargaining, its ownership and its management to provide for the play of our democratic instincts—the most fundamental force in American life.

Regardless of any consequences, I am ready to go down the line to coöperate with anyone to foster this kind of American life, and I am just as ready to go down the line against anyone who tries to destroy this kind of American life. (Applause.)

CHAIRMAN DENNY: *Thank you, Mr. Jackson. Now, we are ready to hear a different point of view. Mr. Willkie, President of the Commonwealth and Southern Corporation, has asked me to state that he cannot and does not attempt to speak for all American industry. His statements and opinions are entirely his own, as I presume are Mr. Jackson's. I take great pleasure in presenting Mr. Wendell L. Willkie.*

MR. WILLKIE: I wonder if it seems strange to any of you tonight that we should be discussing the question of whether or not the government should coöperate with American business. I have an idea that if, from the town meetings of the past, our forefathers should rise to attend this meeting, they would be a little puzzled by such a topic. They might ask, with some surprise, if it was not the function of American government to encourage the development of private enterprise. They would, of course, first be astonished that such a town meeting as this was possible at all— that several million people from all over the land should be gathered together by means of the mysterious network of the air. They would want to be told about this big business of radio manufacture which in fifteen years, by large scale production, has cut the price of its product by three-fourths and sold it to nearly 25,000,000 families. And after they had learned about these things, they would, I think, be even more puzzled as to why, over the facilities made possible by American business genius, we should be discussing whether or not American business, big or little, should be encouraged to proceed.

For several years now we have been listening to a bedtime story telling us that the men who hold office in Washington, are, by their very positions, endowed with a special virtue, that they are men of far vision, and of exceptional ability and capacity. Business men, on the other hand, particularly so-called big business men, are pictured as the ruthless dictators of sprawling industrial empires with no real ability except the talent for collecting money for themselves.

Now, most of you who are listening to this broadcast tonight will remember Joe or Tom or Dick or someone else who left your town and went to the city and made a name for himself in business. Most business leaders today were just such small-town boys. You will remember also other Toms and Dicks and Joes who went into local politics and then into Federal politics, perhaps into one of the many new administrative bureaus in Washington today. On the basis of your own experience, which of these, the business man or the man in politics, wears the longer horns or sports the whiter wings? Would you, from what you know personally, consider the politician to have the greater ability and the more noble character? I tell you quite frankly that I find no halo on the head of either. I have known men in government who were excessively greedy for power and I likewise have known men in business who were excessively greedy for money. But this is not typical of either group, and whatever other monopolies Mr. Jackson may claim to find, I know he has not found, even among government officials, a monopoly on virtue.

But there is another myth that has been handed out to us in recent years, and that is that big business and small business have different and opposing interests. My distinguished companion on the platform has made this a favorite theme of his many speeches. He has warned against government coöperation with big business, maintaining that, to quote his words, "the governmental coöperation which the small business man wants is a different kind."

The fact of the matter is that small business and big business prosper under exactly the same conditions, and the conditions that are harmful to one are harmful to the other. In fact, small business suffers more acutely from such things as heavy taxation, government hostility, and timidity of investment, because it has no reserves with which to preserve itself in time of adversity. Big business supplies a market to small business not only by buying its products but by stimulating the general market; moreover, it furnishes small business with low cost materials and supplies. The two are dependent, one upon the other. When we say that

American industry is prosperous, we mean that the small businesses of America, which comprise the larger part of our industry, are prosperous.

After all, a large corporation is simply a corporation in which, as a rule, the interest is divided among a great many small stockholders. If government succeeds in destroying a large corporation, more people, both stockholders and employees, suffer at one time, that is all. It is not the size that makes a corporation bad or good; it is the way it operates. For example, the government has been currently investigating most of the major industries of the country such as the oil industry, automobiles, telephone and telegraph, utilities, and railroads. These are typical big business industries. What have they achieved? Do they make a good product? Is it sold at a fair price? Does labor receive a fair wage?

Well, every American workingman knows that the highest wages and the best working conditions are found in the large corporations. If the wage and hour bill is passed, the effect on America's big business corporations will be negligible because their wage levels are already above the minimum suggested in the bill. Also, it seems a little ironical for government officials to be lecturing big business on the desirability of low price and large volume because this was the technique which was developed and made possible only by mass production and distribution under the leadership of big business.

The oil industry, for example, is one in which there are a number of very large companies of the kind

Mr. Jackson dislikes. Yet anyone who has driven a car abroad knows that the system of service stations which we take for granted here is duplicated in very few places outside our borders. Although nearly half of what we pay for gasoline represents the government tax, we can still buy it for less than in almost any other place in the world. And, of course, no country pays refinery workers as high a wage as they receive here. In fact, the average hourly wage rates in refineries have increased more than 50 per cent in the past fifteen years while the gasoline price, excluding the tax, has declined by nearly the same amount.

More than 50 per cent of all telephones in the world are in the United States, and they cost the consumer a smaller part of his income than anywhere else.

During the four years ended in 1932, the American automobile industry lost 80 per cent of its business. In one year the industry's net loss was half the cost of the Panama Canal. Yet during that four-year period the industry made a low priced car which was better than the highest priced car in 1926. The public got a better car for considerably less money; and the reduction in price did not come out of the pockets of labor because automobile labor continued to be among the highest paid of all manufacturing industries. Here again, it was big business that made the achievement possible. At a press conference in 1936, President Roosevelt quoted with approval a remark made by Walter P. Chrysler, stating that because of the efficient production methods made possible by the big automobile companies, we could buy a car for $600 today which otherwise would cost $3,500. The President stated at that time that the same methods should be applied to the housing industry.

Of all the industries mentioned, the utility industry, with its enormous demand for additional construction and equipment, is the most important to our economic recovery. And how has it been operated? Since the pre-war years the cost of living has gone up about 40 per cent, and the cost of electricity in this country has gone down by almost exactly the same per cent. *The American consumer pays a smaller part of his income for electricity than the consumers in any country in Europe.* On an average, the American pays nine cents a day for electricity, or less than the government tax on a package and a half of cigarettes.

Since Mr. Jackson has at times employed the usual government argument against the utility holding company, perhaps we should note here that electricity costs less when it is supplied by one of the great utility holding company systems. In every one of the forty-eight states of the United States you will find in operation both the so-called independent utilities which are unaffected by the death sentence of the Utility Holding Company Act, and the utility companies affiliated with holding companies. In forty-four of those forty-eight states the rates of companies in holding company systems are lower than the rates of the independent companies.

For example, Mr. Jackson lives in Washington,

D. C.—at least temporarily—which gets its electricity from one of the companies in the Great North American Holding Company system. A few miles away, operating under identical conditions, is one of those so-called independent companies. The average rate for electric service in the Washington home is three cents per kilowatt-hour. The average rate for this same service in the independent company's territory is four cents, or 33⅓ per cent higher. Because of the low rate of the holding company utility, the home owners of Washington save approximately one and a half million dollars per year in their electricity bill. Which is worth more to the people of that city, a saving of one and a half million dollars on the electricity they use, or the acceptance of a political formula which decrees that mere size is wrong even though it saves money for the people?

I use Washington as an example because Mr. Jackson comes from there. Similar comparisons can be made in almost every state of the Union. Mr. Jackson is mistaken: the Commonwealth and Southern Corporation, of which I have the honor to be President, operates in *eleven* states, five of them in the North. These five northern companies are wholly remote from the Tennessee Valley Authority. The average rate of these companies and our southern companies is lower than that of any utility group in America.

No doubt there have been weaknesses and abuses in all the industries mentioned, and in others, too. Betrayals of trust have stained the record of public

officials as well as of business men. In the period following the great war there was a break-down in both government and private morals. For the first time in
history a member of the Presidential Cabinet was sent
to the penitentiary. Some of those who were in charge
of the hospitals for America's war veterans were in-
dicted, and some convicted, for stealing the very blan-
kets and towels provided for the care of these men
who were injured in their country's service.

Speaking of abuses in his relief program, President
Roosevelt stated: "It should be remembered that in
every big job there are some imperfections. There are
chiselers in every walk of life, there are those in every
industry who are guilty of unfair practices, every profession has its black sheep . . ." If this quotation
from President Roosevelt represents what our attitude
should be toward the mistakes of the few in government—and I think it does—then that should also be
our attitude toward industry. In view of the friendlier
tone of the President's last speeches, I hope that at last
we can have done with the epithets, the calling of names,
the catchwords—catchwords which have been so glibly
used, such as "economic royalists," "Bourbons," "mon-
eyed aristocrats," "banker-control," "holding companies," and the nonsense about "sixty ruling families."

"A good catchword," Justice Oliver Wendell
Holmes said, "can obscure analysis for fifty years."
Today we are very much in need of analysis without
catchwords. The business decline has become so serious that government officials, who at first sought to

minimize it, are now seeking frantically to make big business responsible. Some of these officials allege that the present slump was caused by a few business "strong men," who, like Samson, were willing to destroy themselves in order to pull down the house. They would have us believe that the automobile companies are deliberately trying not to sell cars. They would have us believe that the steel companies which were operating at 90 per cent of capacity are now purposely losing money and operating at 20 per cent of capacity, and that they increased their prices for no reason; whereas, in fact, these prices increased less than wages and costs of materials.

However absurd this charge may be, I see no point in arguing it. I suggest that we have now reached the time when we should stop discussing what caused the depression and should direct our attention to how to cure it. The real cure consists in convincing the millions of small investors throughout America that the government does not intend to continue its attack on American industry, big or little, for it is these investors upon whom industry depends for its funds.

For instance, the utilities need to spend several hundred million dollars for new construction, but they can only raise the money by selling securities. The investor will buy securities only if he thinks that he will get a safe and fair return. He knows that the government is now competing with private industry in the Tennessee Valley by selling electricity at less than cost and charging the loss to the Federal Treasury. He knows that the government is giving money away to municipalities to duplicate existing distribution lines. And he will not invest his money in utilities merely because some one says that the government is competing in only 15 per cent of the country's area.

If there is a smallpox epidemic in a city you cannot convince a man he is in no danger because at the moment only 15 per cent of the city is affected. The investor knows that if the government can compete in 15 per cent of the United States it can compete with any industry, anywhere, and he is not reassured by government efforts to belittle or conceal this competition.

Mr. Jackson has previously spoken of a "strike of capital" against the government. If there is any strike of capital it comes from these millions of small investors, not from the wealthy few. As a matter of fact, because of income tax laws which take up to 83 per cent of a rich man's investment in private enterprise, most of the very rich have been investing more and more in the flood of tax-exempt government securities. It might be helpful to industry, as well as to government revenues, if the government should remove these tax exemptions; but this in and of itself would not be enough. The main problem is to restore the confidence of investors in American business, and to do this will require more than pleasant speaking on the part of government. For several years the government has taken definite action to show its hostility to business. It must now take definite action to demonstrate the sincerity of its desire to coöperate.

I don't think that such coöperation should be difficult. The chief reason why government officials and business men fail to understand each other is because one thinks and speaks the language of politics and emotionalism, while the other thinks and speaks the language of economics and realism. One thinks economic forces can be controlled by politics, while the other realizes that economic forces are more powerful than either government or business. But if we look behind this difference in theory, we can find much upon which we agree in practice.

For example, there seems to be no important disagreement today on the need for a reduction in the undistributed profits tax and the capital gains tax, both of which fall with particular severity upon small businesses and both of which restrict the expansion of industry.

Nor is there any general disagreement as to the principles of the social legislation which has been put upon the statute books in recent years. Time has revealed both the virtues and the weaknesses of these laws. The proposal now is simply one of eliminating the weaknesses; of modifying those restrictions upon the buying and selling of securities that hamper the investment of funds; of readjusting the Social Security Act to a pay-as-you-go basis, so that the money paid by the people for social security is used only for that purpose; of protecting the rights of both capital and labor in the promotion of collective bargaining; of getting rid of intermediate holding companies in the utility industry without declaring a "death sentence" upon all of them.

Six weeks ago I left with the President a memorandum suggesting a solution of the utility program—a solution which did not ask for less Federal regulation of utilities, but did ask for an end to unfair government competition and unfair government destruction of the property of American citizens. I am still hopeful that that memorandum will provide a basis upon which the utilities may be permitted to go ahead with their construction plans.*

Now, is there anything in this outline of a possible relationship between government and business that is not in the interest of the ill-housed, the ill-fed and the ill-clad? Is there anything here that is opposed to the social regulation of business? Does this attitude imply that business is "ganging up" on government, or that a few corporations are attempting to swallow up all American industry?

In such a time as this, when we see the relief rolls lengthening again and the price of farm products declining, when many of us are discouraged and when the road to recovery seems long, surely business and government should put an end to the bitterness of recent years and sit down in conference like reasonable men with mutual tolerance and respect. But the purpose of this conference must not only be to plan intelligently for the future, but to review those laws which have been

---

* This memorandum was never discussed with Mr. Willkie by the President.

passed—to see whether they cannot be so modified as to stimulate business activity, without removing any of the appropriate social controls. And above all, while these conferences are proceeding, the American people should be spared the confusion of hearing what one government official says in friendship today denied by another in hostility tomorrow.

At this critical point in our nation's history, it would seem fitting that business and government should bear in mind the warning which Abraham Lincoln gave to the two factions into which this country was dividing at the time of his first inaugural address. "I am loath to close," he said; "we are not enemies, but friends. We must not be enemies." (Applause.)

CHAIRMAN DENNY: Mr. Willkie has taken a little more than his allotted time and as the clock is our yardstick of fair play, Mr. Jackson is entitled to six minutes, which he tells me he would rather waive in favor of the questions. Now, please save your own time and don't take up time applauding and demonstrating. Let's have your questions. Questions, please!

MAN: Mr. Jackson, you made reference to a statement made by Mr. Knudsen. I chanced to read his testimony before the Senate Committee today. He made a statment before the Committee today that the reason the sale of automobiles had declined was not because the people were thrown out of work and had no money to buy, but that even though they had the money they were afraid to buy because they might not have jobs in the future. In other words, there is a period of uncertainty ahead which has reduced purchasing power.

MR. JACKSON: Unfortunately, I have not read Mr. Knudsen's testimony, and I don't like to comment on testimony that I haven't heard. I did read his statement as quoted in the *New York Times* at the time that the 30,000 men were discharged, and I am not surprised if as a result of that there is a good deal of uncertainty in the hearts and minds of a good many workingmen as to whether their jobs will last. (Applause.)

MAN: I would like to ask Mr. Willkie whether big business or small business is more likely to hire labor spies? (Applause.)

CHAIRMAN DENNY: Mr. Willkie, do you want to comment on that?

MR. WILLKIE: Certainly. Being a member of big business who never hired a labor spy in my life, I don't know the motive that actuates either a big or little business, and I would repudiate the act by both big business and little business. (Applause.)

MAN: Mr. Jackson, how do you reconcile the New Deal program for farmers to cut production to raise prices with its plan of increasing industrial production to lower prices?

MR. JACKSON: Every person who has ever lived upon a farm knows that there is an essential difference in the method of production on a farm and the production in a factory. No farmer can control his production unless he can control the weather, and that is one of the things we haven't gotten around to regulate yet. (Laughter and applause.)   Factory production is controlled and can be controlled, which makes an entirely different matter.

MAN: Mr. Jackson, don't we the people fear an undue concentration in government as much or more than we fear this concentration in business?

MR. JACKSON: Yes, sir, we do fear it.   We do fear it.   And the American people never would concentrate government if they didn't have to concentrate government to regulate the concentration of big business. (Applause, cheers, and cries of "No.")   How can a single state regulate Mr. Willkie?

VOICE: That might be in Italy or Germany, but it isn't that in the United States of America. (Applause.)

MAN: Mr. Willkie, what accounts for the Canadian electric rates being so much less than the rates of the utility companies on this side of the Niagara?

MR. WILLKIE: I was just hoping somebody would ask me that question.   (Laughter and applause.) The difference is that the American utility companies are now paying up to 20 per cent of their gross revenue in taxes, while the public plants in Canada pay no taxes, except a minor amount of taxes on real estate.   (Applause.)

MAN: Mr. Willkie, you mentioned in your address that the large corporations pay a higher wage scale and have better working conditions than smaller concerns. Is that not by reason of the fact of the large labor turnover in large corporations?

MR. WILLKIE: First, I disagree with you about the facts. In the utility business, there is practically no turnover in labor. Most of our employees have been with us for more than ten years. I would say that the policy of American industry, as is well illustrated by the attitude of General Motors, has been to attempt to make the production regular so that men may be employed as much as possible throughout the year and reduce to a minimum the turnover in labor. (Applause.)

MAN: Mr. Willkie, what do you think the attitude of the government should be towards the cement industry which controls prices throughout the country?

MR. WILLKIE: There is on the statute books the anti-trust statute. You have seen demonstrating tonight one of the ablest lawyers in the United States who is charged with the prosecution of any violation of that statute. I would suggest that Mr. Jackson go to work, if there is anything wrong in the cement industry or in any other industry with reference to monopolistic practices. (Applause.)

MAN: I should like to ask Mr. Jackson what he thinks of the undistributed profits surtax?

MR. JACKSON: The undistributed profits tax undoubtedly is in need of amendment in several particulars, particularly as it affects small industry. (Applause.) I want to say to you that I believe in the undistributed profits tax in the main. I know that the representations that have been made that corporate surpluses are a cushion against depression are not true, because General Motors, when it laid off 30,000 men, had over $400,000,000 of corporate surplus. (Applause.)

WOMAN: Mr. Jackson said that farm production could not be controlled. Why did the government attempt it in the case of cotton?

MR. JACKSON: The most the government attempted to do was to place a maximum of production and to avoid the creation of a surplus which could not be handled since the foreign markets had fallen away, due to the fact that we had quit sending foreign money abroad with which they could buy our products. (Cries of "No.")

WOMAN: Mr. Jackson, if the government continues its expansion program in the power field, what will happen to the billions of dollars invested in stocks and bonds now held by our insurance companies, investment trusts, estates, and the public?

MR. JACKSON: The government of the United States has never attempted to destroy the power industry. (Cry of "Not much.") The government of the United States wants the power industry to furnish power at rates that are fair to the public as well as to the utility companies. (Applause.) Long before I was in politics I pointed out to the utility industry in an address to the American Bar Association utility lawyers that the trouble with the power industry was that it was issuing too many securities called "power securities" that had little relation to power and none to security. (Cry of "Right" and applause.)

MAN: Mr. Jackson, do you think the fair way to get

lower electric rates is to subsidize municipal competition with 50 per cent grants and free taxation?

MR. JACKSON: I don't think the question of fairness enters into it. I don't know that it is necessarily fair for two policemen to arrest one crook. But, if the Government of the United States is going to carry out its power policy by competitive methods, because we have seen the methods of regulation due to the big holding companies' control break down, it must use ordinary competitive methods. (Boos and applause.)

WOMAN: Mr. Willkie, is it not true that the rates of Commonwealth and Southern are the lowest because of pressure from TVA? (Applause.)

MR. WILLKIE: As I said, we operate in eleven states, five in the North and six in the South. Our rate schedules in our major northern companies are almost identical with the rate schedules in our southern companies, only those in the North are slightly lower. The Tennessee Valley Authority is building competitive lines, and the Federal Government is giving 45 per cent absolutely free with which to duplicate existing utility systems in Tennessee. The average rate of the Tennessee Electric Power Company is less than three cents, which is twenty-five to thirty per cent below the national average, and those properties will be destroyed and the investors will lose their money if this policy, which Mr. Jackson recognizes has no element of fairness in it, is not discontinued. (Applause.)

MAN: Mr. Jackson, is the aim of the New Deal ultimately to nationalize all the public utilities?

MR. JACKSON: I should say, No. I haven't heard of its nationalizing any public utilities. (Applause.)

MAN: Has it occurred to Mr. Jackson that the price government power operations quote does not include the interest on the capital invested in the form of the taxpayers' money nor for provision for amortization of the debt? In other words, an incomplete balance sheet is presented to the American public and endorsed as bona fide by the Government. What is the difference between this procedure and Mr. Insull's? (Laughter and applause.)

MR. JACKSON: I am not an accountant, and if I were, I wouldn't attempt to give an answer to that question in the time that is allowed here. I don't know the details of the accounting of TVA, and I don't know the details of the accounting of private utilities.

CHAIRMAN DENNY: *Thank you, Mr. Jackson, we must close now. I hope that all who are listening in as groups will continue their discussions as profitably as I know we are going to continue it here among ourselves. (Applause.)*

IDLE MONEY—IDLE MEN

IDLE MONEY—IDLE MEN

Reprinted from
THE SATURDAY EVENING POST,
June 17th, 1939.

IDLE MONEY—IDLE MEN

By *Wendell Willkie*

EVERY Friday morning the newspapers of the country publish in their financial sections a short "statement of condition" of member banks of the Federal Reserve System. The statement is put out by the Federal Reserve Board in Washington. It contains in particular a figure entitled, "Member Bank Reserve Balances."

Probably 99 per cent of the people of this country have never noted that figure and would not understand it if they had. But economists, businessmen responsible for corporation policy, and Government financial officials pay close attention to it. Member banks must keep a certain reserve, against their deposits, in the Federal Reserve Bank in their district. The amount of this reserve above the legal requirements is called "excess." It is, perhaps, the best single indication of how much money is available as a possible base for credit expansion in this country—credit which might be used to finance business, but which is lying idle.

In 1929, the year before the depression, the excess reserves in member banks averaged about $43,000,000. On April 26, 1939—in the week in which this article was written—they reached an all-time peak of $4,120,-000,000. In other words, more than $4,000,000,000 which could have been used as a basis for credit expansion was lying idle in the banks of the country—almost 100 times the average amount lying idle in 1929.

Why wasn't this money being used? Doesn't business need it? Does industry in this country have all the modern plants and equipment which it requires, so that it does not want any additional capital for these purposes? Aren't the banks and the investors interested in investing their money so they can earn a return on it? Of course, everyone knows the answer to that. Banks cannot make a living unless they can put their deposits to work. The investor does not want to bury his money in a hole in the ground; he wants an income from it, as long as he can get it with reasonable safety; and as for industry, it is badly in need of capital equipment.

If it could get the money, it could employ several millions of men in replacing obsolete machinery and enlarging its plants. For example, the Brookings Institution estimated that in 1936 between twenty-five and thirty billions of dollars would be needed for durable goods alone to make up the deficiency that had accumulated to that date, largely because of postponed repairs and replacements. The Brookings Institution is not a political organization. It simply investigates and reports the facts as it finds them. For the period since 1936 probably fifteen billion dollars should be added to that figure, which would make a total of at least forty billions of dollars needed for the manufacture or construction of durable goods.

The deficiency in durable goods is particularly high because in a depression durable goods—by which we mean factories, heavy machinery, buildings and long-lasting materials—can be postponed. But non-durable goods—that is, consumers' goods—are much more difficult to postpone. As long as we have any money at all, we will wear clothing and eat, even in a depression.

It has been estimated that if industry could get this money that it needs and put it to work, it would provide employment directly for some 3,000,000 men in operating plant and equipment, and for some 6,000,000 to 9,000,000 men in the service industries. Since we have a total unemployment today of nearly 11,000,000 —close to what we had at the low point of 1933—those figures sound interesting.

On the one hand, then, there is an enormous amount of idle money. On the other hand, there is industry which is very much in need of that money for capital expenditures that would create jobs.

This country's depression can be solved whenever we can bring those two factors together. If we lived under a dictatorship, the dictator would order the banks to loan the money and the corporations to borrow and expend it. If we lived under the Russian system, both the supply of capital and the industries would be socialized. But both of those systems, as the very basis of their functioning, require the subordination of all personal liberty to the state. The question is, can we cause our great reservoir of free capital to flow into the channels of industry under a democracy? If we can, our democratic system will be preserved.   If we cannot, then our democracy will vanish in the chaos of national bankruptcy through a continually rising, unbalanced Federal budget, or through its overthrow by those unsupplied with the necessities of life.

What are the difficulties?

You can answer that question partly by asking it of yourself. Perhaps you were planning to buy a new car this year, or a new radio. Perhaps you had some thought of buying a small place in the country, or, if you already have one, of fixing up the barn. But now you hesitate and wonder if you ought to spend the money at this time. One thing that holds you back is, of course, the talk of a world war.* But though that has been disquieting, it hasn't been—in this country— the major consideration. The real thing that bothers you is a certain general unrest and uncertainty which you feel all about you. The memory of that 10 per cent pay cut a few years ago and then a second 10 per cent is still a sobering thought, even though most of it has been restored. Your employer is beginning to seem worried again. It is probably wiser to wait awhile and not add any unnecessary commitments to your budget just at this time

Now, if you and I feel that way about our personal expenditures, you can imagine that the feeling would be intensified tenfold if we were investing in somebody else's enterprise, or if we were executives of a corporation, responsible to employees and stockholders. At

* Written in April, 1939.

least, when we spend our own money for something of our own, we still have the thing if conditions go bad—provided we do not buy it on a shoestring. But when we put the money in somebody else's business, over which we have no control, that seems a little more risky. And if we are running a business, the possibility of failing to make enough money to cover the proposed expenditure is disturbing. In short, it is fear—fear as to what the Government is going to do, fear as to what may happen to industry—that has kept the investor from providing business with capital and has prevented the re-equipment of established industry and the launching of new business ventures.

Four years ago I made a speech in Washington about *The New Fear*. I pointed out that the President of the United States in his inaugural address had given us new courage in a dark hour by telling us that "the only thing we have to fear is fear itself." The American people of every class—employees, employers and unemployed—responded with eager hearts to that appeal and put into the President's hands almost unlimited powers to meet the emergency. But after two years had passed—and a great many laws—it became clear that something was holding us back—and that was fear. But it was a different kind of fear from that which the President talked about—it was the fear of Government itself.

That was four years ago, and the fear has not abated. Instead, business is increasingly aware that the Government is gradually taking over the functions of private enterprise. And the Government is accomplishing this by three methods, all of them closely related to one another—regulation, Government competition and the policy of "spend and spend, tax and tax."

I. GOVERNMENT REGULATION

Regulation has become an exceedingly complicated process. The Government of the United States now issues a directory of Government agencies—a new publication, never necessary before. It is a loose-leaf directory, so that additions and changes can be constantly made. It lists some eighty departments, bureaus and commissions now carrying on the Government's activities. These are executive agencies. Some of them may be consolidated under the proposed reorganization plan, but, of course, their functions will still continue. They have nothing to do with Congress. Many of these new agencies have been created to administer the new laws regulating American industry; some of the others are for the purpose of competing with industry.

Lawmaking isn't so simple as it was in the old days. For one thing, we are trying to regulate industries which operate in different sections of the country, where wage levels, housing conditions, markets, prices and everything else, including the weather, are different. When we pass a law of that scope now, we have to set up a commission to administer it. Congress passed the Securities Exchange Act, for example, and set up the Securities and Exchange Commission. It passed the Wage and Hour Act and set up the Wage and Hour Division in the Department of Labor. It passed the National Labor Relations Act and set up the National Labor Relations Board. It passed the Federal Communications Act and set up the Federal Communications Commission. And so on. Of course, we had already inherited a couple of commissions, like the Federal Trade Commission and the Federal Power Commission, from the past.

Many of these laws were passed with the desire to punish. We wanted to punish industry for past abuses and we wanted—quite rightly—to make certain that these abuses would not recur. We should be willing now, however, to re-examine these laws to determine not only what they have prevented but what they have contributed.

There used to be a saying among the American colonists that "there was no good Indian except a dead Indian." Some of our legislators seem to feel the same way about business and, as a result, they aren't concerned as to how much business is killed off by their proposals. Since most of the people in this country live by industry, however, we don't want it killed; not even in the interest of making it virtuous. We want it to be a living, helpful force in our lives, even if it may continue to have imperfections.

But I am not considering here the modifications which these laws may require in order that their objectives may be more fully achieved. I am considering the method of administration by commissions. Since the laws are concerned with very complex activities, the administrative commissions were probably necessary. Laws governing wages and hours or social security or public utilities or any other vast national activity cannot possibly prescribe for every situation that might arise; and so these commissions are empowered to make the rules that should apply. Obviously, this is dangerous. It involves a subtle transfer of Government power. The rules of these executive commissions are superseding the laws of Congress.

From the standpoint of a businessman, there is a very important difference between a congressional law and a commission rule. The congressional law is fixed. It is down in black and white. It is the same for everybody, and anybody can find out what it is. A commission rule may be changed in twenty-four hours. It need not be on paper at all. It can be varied to fit different cases. Under the present commission regulation of industry, therefore, we have a highly personal form of government—a government by caprice in which the good will of a commission chairman may have a considerable effect upon you and your business.

The present network of Government bureaus regulating the activities of employer and employee thus imposes a grave responsibility upon the regulators. The members of the commissions who hold in their hands such extraordinary power must exercise it so justly that business and the public will have confidence in their administration. Personal prejudice must not enter into their decisions, and political influence must not warp their integrity.

II. Government Competition

Of course, this strict Government regulation of industry has made it much easier for the second step in the Government's invasion of industry—competition. A man with one hand tied behind his back has a poor chance in the ring with an unbound opponent. In the past few years various "Government corporations" have been established, engaging in all kinds of financial and even industrial activities. These Government corporations run on separate budgets, maintain separate books and actually issue their own Government-guaranteed securities.

There is, of course, the Tennessee Valley Authority, as an outstanding illustration of a competitive Government enterprise. There are also such quasi-banking agencies as the RFC, the Commodity Credit Corporation, the Housing Administration, the Farm Mortgage Corporation, the Federal Home Loan Banks, the National Mortgage Association, and others, which have budgets of their own and issue their own securities, but are, of course, Government corporations. By organizing them in this manner, the Government does not have to include the indebtedness of these corporations in its regular statement of the public debt.

Personally, I feel very strongly about this question of Government competition because I have been fighting it now for five years and have lost one company in the process.   On June twentieth, the Commonwealth & Southern System, of which I am the head, will turn over to the Government one of its best companies, the Tennessee Electric Power Company.*   This company had a total asset value of about $108,000,000.   It served 124,000 customers, at an average domestic rate of two and three-quarter cents per kilowatt-hour, one of the lowest rates in the country.   It paid almost $3,000,000 in taxes each year.   It was a good company and never had any trouble with its customers, and it had a real future in the development of Tennessee.

But the Government organized the Tennessee Valley Authority, which used Government money to build power dams and generating plants in that state.   The Tennessee Electric Power Company offered to buy that Government power and redistribute it at rates to be fixed by the Federal Government, but the Government didn't want to sell it to the company.   The Government wanted its own power system.   It tried to persuade municipalities to set up their own distribution systems by offering to give them 45 per cent of the money and to lend them the balance at a low interest rate.

No one could compete with competition of that kind. As owners of the Tennessee Electric Power Company, we had no choice; we were forced to sell that company to the Government, and in June a private enterprise,

* The Tennessee Electric Power Company was transferred to the Government on August 15, 1939.

started thirty-five years ago, will become Government property.

The question now disturbing the utility industry is: What company will be next to go? We have been asking the Government for some time to set a limit beyond which it will not compete with private enterprise, but, as yet, it has failed to agree to set any such limit. In the meantime, no utility in the Tennessee Valley can raise any capital, and all utility investors fear for the safety of their investments.

Because the utility industry is such an important one in this country, this has had a depressing effect on all industry. But businessmen generally, as is perhaps only human, have been saying: "Well, that's tough luck for the utilities, but at least it hasn't hit my business." For several years I have been trying to point out to them that in the long run they will be wrong, but they have felt that Government competition with private industry is clearly unconstitutional and that, when the worst comes to the worst, the courts will protect them.

Unfortunately for this theory, two Supreme Court decisions within the past few months have, in effect, denied to industry the right of protection against competition by the Government.

In the case of the Tennessee Electric Power Company and others versus the TVA, decided by the United States Supreme Court on January 30, 1939, the public utilities raised the question as to whether the United States, through its agency, the TVA, could compete with private enterprise in the electricity business. The

TVA itself admitted, and the Supreme Court assumed, that public utilities were damaged by this competition.

But the Supreme Court expressly refused to answer this question of the constitutionality of TVA competition. In its own words, it said: "For reasons about to be stated, we do not consider or decide the issue thus mooted." The court held that competition by the TVA, even though unauthorized by the Constitution, could not be challenged by the utilities, because the latter had no right to be free of competition, even illegal competition.

Previous to that, the Alabama Power Company had challenged the constitutional right of the Federal Government to give loans and gifts to cities for the construction of competing electric distribution systems. The Supreme Court, in that case, also had decided that the private power companies could not question the constitutionality of this, even though they were damaged thereby.

In short, these two cases mean that a privately owned corporation has no standing to challenge either the direct business competition of the Federal Government or indirect competition made possible by Federal gifts to state agencies, however unconstitutional the competition may be.

If this gives the Government the right to compete with the utilities, which must by their very nature, as admitted by both enemies and friends, be relatively free of competition, how much more right does it give to the Government to compete with other industries, where

competition is accepted as a desirable matter of course?
The Government, for example, might decide to manufacture trucks and automobiles because these were
needed for the transportation of the Army. The Government would build its plants and get its equipment—
with the taxpayers' money and, of course, free of taxation itself—and if it started then to manufacture trucks
and cars and sell the surplus in competition with private
industry, no private corporation would be able to challenge the constitutionality of that practice.

So, when businessmen commiserate with me because
Government competition has cost us one of our companies, I am inclined to warn them, very frankly, that
they may be next on the list. Their protection lies
now, not in the courts but in the people. It is the
people, finally, who will determine whether or not free
private enterprise in this country shall give way in favor of a business managed by bureaus in Washington.

III. SPENDING AND TAXATION

*In addition to regulation and competition by the
Government, the third method by which Government is
taking over the functions of private enterprise is by
discouraging the American investor from putting his
money into industry. This is being done in two ways—
by spending and by taxing.* In the past three or four
years we have been trying to buy our way into prosperity with Government money. I am not talking now
about such normal Government expenditures as those

amounts usually spent on roads, schools, Army and Navy, police, post office, and so on. Nor am I talking about the expenditures necessary to keep people from starving. I am discussing that special and extra type of Government spending which is designed solely for the purpose of recovery—what we call "pump-priming."

I am beginning to suspect that a lot of people use the word "pump-priming" without really knowing what it means. But, of course, every boy who has ever been on a farm should understand it. When you went to get the horses out of the barn in the morning, you led them over to the pump and filled the water buckets. But first you poured a glass of water down the pump to get it started. That little glass of water and a few quick strokes of the handle were all that you needed before the pump started to flow.

Government pump-priming doesn't seem to work that way. The amounts poured down the pump are not small; they are enormous. And still the water doesn't flow. In other words, we have today nearly 11,000,000 unemployed—and we had 12,000,000 unemployed in 1932. In the meantime, the Government debt gets bigger and bigger, and the budget deficit, for the decade 1931-40, will amount to more than $27,000,-000,000. That is enough to make anyone uneasy, but the deficit itself is not so disturbing as the fact that these large Government expenditures are driving private investment out of business.

Now, at first thought, you might think that it makes

little difference where the money comes from, as long as the money is there. But, of course, there is a big difference between how the Government uses its money and how you use yours. You don't put your money into a business unless you think it is a paying proposition. But the Government does not have to earn a return on its money. It spends it chiefly for non-productive purposes, including all kinds of civic projects. Some of these are very desirable, but the point is, they do not create the jobs that private money, spent for productive purposes, would create—chiefly in the production of durable goods, which, as I have already pointed out, is the category where there has been practically no recovery. We are in a situation today where the Government expenditures have become so high and taxes have increased to such an extent that private industry and private investment have been scared into hiding.

I have stayed off the subject of taxes as long as I could, but it had to come up sometime. The average American certainly doesn't like taxes, but he knows he isn't going to get rid of them, and, on the whole, doesn't want to talk about them. It is not taxes, *per se,* that I am criticizing here. It is the kind of tax that has been imposed.

First of all, there is this business of "soaking the rich." This has the same objective, but, of course, is less harmful than the various share-the-wealth proposals. Under these share-the-wealth proposals, if we took the salary of everybody who received $150,000 and up, for example, and divided it among all the people in this country—— No, that wouldn't do, because the amount each would get would be only fifteen cents. So let's say that $5000 is enough for anybody to receive, and everything above that amount should be divided. That doesn't work very well, either, because all we would get would be $2.32 a month. So, instead of doing anything as drastic as that, we set a very high tax on large incomes. If a man has an income of $1,000,000 for example—and there are still two or three of these left—the state and Federal governments will promptly take 84 per cent of it. If a man has an income of $100,000, the state and Federal governments will promptly take 40 per cent of it.

Our attitude might be: Well, who cares? Those men can afford it. So, for good measure, we add a capital-gains tax whereby everybody, rich or poor, who makes any profit out of a transaction—investing in a business or in property or in securities—pays a tax on it; but if he happens to lose—and since only one-third of the established businesses are successful, he is more apt to lose than win—he may deduct only a small portion of his losses.

By both of these actions—by too high a tax on incomes and by a tax on capital gains—we are forcing the man who can afford to put his money into industry to put it into tax-exempt securities or into something other than the new business ventures which the country needs. As the Comptroller of the state of New York recently stated, there are two kinds of money. There is investment money that takes no chance, that is invested in seasoned gilt-edged securities, and then there is the pioneering money that goes to build up new industry and create new jobs. It is the latter kind of money that the Government tax program is destroying.

The effects of excessive taxation can be illustrated in a very simple manner. Let us take the case of a miller in a small village who buys ten bushels of wheat a day from a farmer and grinds them into flour. He needs, let us say, four bushels for himself. He pays a tax of two bushels to the town to take care of the poor and the aged. He agrees to give two bushels to a man who is to paint his house, and two bushels to the local dry-goods man in part payment for a suit of clothes. The town fathers, however, decide that they need more, that they should exact a larger tribute from the miller, and they ask him for four bushels a day. He naturally resents it, but he has to pay. He still needs four bushels for himself, so, in order to get it, he cancels his order for the clothes. This process continues until finally the miller decides that he might just as well take only enough bushels of wheat to support himself and his family and to pay the taxes. He therefore (1) reduces his purchases from the farmer; (2) cancels his agreement with the painter; and (3) calls off his trade with the dry-goods store. In other words, he curtails his own production, and thereby adds to the town's unemployment problem.

Of course, the tax on the undistributed profits of corporations has much the same effect in preventing corporations from putting their money into new plants and new equipment. And that is another tax that reduces the potential number of jobs. No one has stated the effects of excessive taxation better than President Roosevelt himself, who said, in October, 1932:

> Taxes are paid in the sweat of every man who labors because they are a burden on production and can be paid only by production. If excessive, they are reflected in idle factories, tax-sold farms, and hence in hordes of the hungry tramping the streets and seeking jobs in vain. Our workers may never see a tax bill, but they pay in deductions from wages, in increased cost of what they buy, or (as now) in broad cessation of employment. There is not an unemployed man—there is not a struggling farmer— whose interest in this subject is not direct and vital.

Government regulation, Government competition and Government discouragement of investment are the three elements that compose the fear which dominates the businessman and the investor today. And if we balance up the books, where are we?

1. We still have those 11,000,000 unemployed. Nobody can get away from that fact.

2. We have lying idle in the banks several billion dollars of money for investment.

3. We have a need for all that money, and more, to be spent for the capital expenditures of industry.

And if we can add Item No. 2 to Item No. 3, then we can largely get rid of Item No. 1. When the people of America feel strongly enough about it, they will force the Government to abandon those hostile policies that make this achievement impossible.

BRACE UP, AMERICA!

BRACE UP, AMERICA!

Reprinted from

THE ATLANTIC MONTHLY

June, 1939.

BRACE UP, AMERICA!

By *Wendell Willkie*

FROM the way the reformers handle the word "profit," one might conclude that there was something wrong about it. Fortunately the dictionary confirms our suspicion that the word signifies a *desirable* condition. It is defined as "any accession or increase of good from labor or exertion, comprehending the acquisition of anything valuable, intellectual or corporeal, temporal or spiritual."

In this fundamental sense, the word "profit" applies as much to the birth of a baby as to a pay envelope at the end of the week. It is the hope of youth and the reward of age. It is the mainspring of all human activity and the dynamic force behind the progress of all civilization. We work for a greater good, both for ourselves and for others, and the function of an organized state is to encourage that ambition.

Within the past several years, various official spokesmen have belittled both the desirability and the possibility of profits. We have been told that the frontiers are gone and that there are few opportunities as compared with the old days. We have been advised that security is more important than profit. And this intellectual disdain of profit making has been supplemented by legislation which renders it exceedingly difficult.

Some of the leaders in this campaign honestly believe that American industry has expanded too greatly, and that further expansion should be retarded; some of them are motivated by a desire to punish industry for the abuses of the past; some of them, in their zeal for reform, fail to realize that, while a strait-jacket will keep a man out of trouble, it is not a suitable garment in which to work.

Whatever the motive, the result of these efforts is all too apparent: after six years of strict regulation and taxation of industry, we have as many people unemployed as at the beginning of the period. That is the grim and inescapable fact. The reluctance of business men to accept wholeheartedly the reformer's point of view is not a result of any lack of humanitarianism. The intelligent among them are as anxious as the political reformer to see wages at a high level, to enhance the security of the aged and unemployed, and to maintain honest markets for securities and commodities. Such men, however, ask in all sincerity how these desirable conditions can be achieved without impairing the industrial system that pays the wages, employs the workers, manufactures the products, and utilizes the investment.

When industry has a chance to make profits, it expands and employs more men; when it is unprofitable, it reduces employment and curtails its operations. Fortunately, with a little will—even a little *good will*—we can remove all of those artificial barriers to profit making without too much difficulty; and we can do this without upsetting any of the economic reforms of the past few years.

Three conditions are primarily responsible for the extraordinary economic achievements of the American people. We were, of course, lucky in coming to a land where the natural resources were abundant. We were even luckier to come to it at such a time and under such circumstances that it could be developed as a whole, before it was chopped up into small competing territories as in Europe. This meant that we were not only rich in raw materials but blessed with the greatest free-trade area in the world. We could ship our goods from one coast of the continent to the other without ever paying a tariff or passing a customs inspection.

To these physical conditions our forefathers added what might be called a spiritual one: a faith in individual initiative and free enterprise. When our forefathers said "freedom," they did not mean simply freedom of speech, freedom of press, or freedom of religion. They meant economic freedom as well. They were strong believers in the desirability of encouraging business enterprise.

This item of economic freedom has not loomed sufficiently large in the dossier on liberty maintained by the professional apostles. Tainted, perhaps, with that slight social inferiority which, as mentioned, seems to attach to the word "profits," economic freedom has less standing than its intellectual and moral counterparts.

This, however, is an invalid discrimination. In the end, all forms of freedom stand or fall together. You cannot have freedom of religion without freedom of speech—or vice versa. You cannot have either one of them without free business enterprise. For the alternative, a planned economy, calls for rigid control of prices and production; and this control in turn leads to the suppression of civil freedom.

Presumably our forefathers were aware of this interdependence of liberties. Certainly they seemed to recognize the necessity of encouraging economic enterprise for the sake of popular welfare. The results have been extraordinary, although the statistics are so worn by use that they have lost the stamp of their significance. Today we have 6 per cent of the world's area and 7 per cent of its population, but more than 45 per cent of its wealth. We can summarize our economic achievement, without going into detail, by stating that we have the highest real wages, the shortest working hours, and the greatest percentage of home ownership on earth.

I believe that this achievement was possible only because men in America were encouraged to take risks; the entrepreneur was given a chance to profit; the inventor and the investor alike were willing to assume the hazard of loss because they were not denied the chance of gain. Industry went to work in an atmosphere as brisk and stimulating as a New England autumn.

Today the atmosphere is spiritless. The Secretary

of the Treasury recently epitomized it when he spoke
of the "What's the use?" attitude of business men—
not the big business men alone, but the small ones as
well: the shopkeeper, the local mill owner, the man with
fifty shares of stock carefully diversified among five
companies. And the cause of this melancholia in a
naturally spirited people is found in those legislative
policies that discourage the use of private capital for
the development of industry and prevent the re-employment of millions looking for jobs.

These policies are principally as follows: (1) government spending on an enormous scale; (2) wage fixing
and payroll taxing which increase the costs of employment; (3) personal and corporate taxes which penalize
investment and expansion; (4) capricious interference
with industry by regulatory commissions.

I

*The theory that the government can spend its way
into prosperity has two evil consequences.* Of these two
evils the lesser is the better-known—the unbalanced
budget. In the past ten years our total government
deficit has mounted to over 27 billion dollars. The
figures are so large that, like the sky overhead, they
make no particular impression as to size. The deficit
for the fiscal year will be nearly four billion dollars,
and the estimated deficit in 1940 is only slightly less
than that figure.

Most of us, of course, do not know what national

bankruptcy means; we have a sturdy faith in the American dollar and we cannot imagine its ever being used for wallpaper, like the old German mark; but we are vaguely uneasy when we contemplate the prolongation of this deficit policy. At all events we are beginning to realize that deficits mean high taxes which somebody— either we or our children—will have to pay.

But the deficit itself is not the worst feature of the government's spending policy. The worst feature is the fact that government spending drives private capital out of industry and prevents exactly the kind of investment which recovery demands—namely, voluntary spending *for productive purposes* by the people who have money to invest. As in Gresham's law— "bad money drives out good money"—these huge indiscriminate government expenditures, many of them in direct competition with business, have scared private investment into hiding.

One of the leading advocates of government spending is Marriner Eccles, Chairman of the Federal Reserve Board. He has attempted to assure the private investor (although he should know better—and perhaps he does) that the extent of government spending is no cause for alarm because it has merely taken the place of private spending, and the total debt, public and private, is no larger today than in 1929. It is just because government spending *has* taken the place of private spending, however, that there is reason for alarm.

As Senator Byrd has ably pointed out, there is a very

great difference between the public debt and the private debt. The public debt is created by the government and not directly by the people who pay it. The private debt, on the other hand, is voluntarily created by people who expect to pay off the debt. The public debt is created primarily for nonproductive purposes—relief payments, military expenditures, civic projects, and so forth. But the private debt is created for purposes of industrial production—chiefly for the production of durable goods, which represent the most conspicuously retarded of our country's industries.

The private debt has declined each year of the depression, since 1930, and the total decline amounts to eleven and a half billion dollars. The federal debt, on the other hand, has increased each year of this period, and the total increase amounts to twenty-two billion dollars.

Now some of this government money was constructively used. It helped to stimulate retail business activities; it built some very useful public works; it helped to restore the morale of the young unemployed through the work done by the Civilian Conservation Corps. But this type of spending tends to be wasteful and unproductive because the government does not have to get a return on its money; it does not have to consider the economic soundness of its projects; unlike private capital, it does not face the imperative necessity of earning its way. Moreover, government property does not pay a tax; and to make up for this exemption the tax on private property must be increased. Since the government through the TVA has purchased the Tennessee Electric Power Company, for example, the state and municipalities of Tennessee will lose $3,500,000 in taxes which can be recovered only by increasing the taxes on the citizens and their business.

But any theoretical argument as to government spending versus private spending should be largely unnecessary, since the failure of government spending is only too obvious. Government spending has not provided jobs for the 10,000,000 unemployed. It has failed to increase the national income to a point where budget balancing is possible. It has failed to stimulate the industries producing durable goods. It has undermined financial confidence, doubled the public debt, and enormously increased taxation.

II

Fixing wages and taxing payrolls have increased the costs of employment, and thus reduced the number of those employed.

In this country we have long been rightly proud of the relatively high wages paid to American workers as compared with the workers abroad. There were, of course, plenty of inequities in the situation. There were many sections where sweatshop wages were paid, and many where the employee had no voice whatsoever in determining his working conditions. The present Administration's proposals to improve these conditions met not only with the endorsement of the increasingly strong labor unions, but with that of the general public. Unfortunately, when wage increases are arbitrarily set by law, they may hurt the American laborer instead of helping him.

Wages are paid out of what industry can get for its output. When industry is confidently engaged in the development of new products and the improvement of existing ones, when it has ample capital from private investors to finance its needs, and when there is an active market for its products—then we have a condition which tends to increase wages. If, however, wages are artificially raised—either by government legislation or by union activities—beyond the level which industry can meet out of its current operations, then there is an almost immediate drop in employment, and the total laboring income declines. That is the basic fallacy in the idea that wage increases are automatically desirable because they increase the laborer's purchasing power.

The NRA constitutes the most startling example of the effects of arbitrary methods of handling wages. From March to July, 1933, immediately preceding the NRA, industrial production showed an increase of 69 per cent. Then, under the NRA, hours were shortened and wages were arbitrarily raised. Labor costs enormously increased, and there was a drop in industrial production (from July to December, 1933) of 25 per cent. The Director of Research of the NRA estimates, for example, that by reason of the minimum wage provisions of the lumber codes about 500,000 Negro workers in the South were on relief in 1934.

That is why the labor unions should not take the benefits of the Wages and Hours Act for granted, but should closely observe its operations.

Very serious disturbances have resulted in Puerto Rico as a result of the enactment of even the minimum-wage standard of 25 cents an hour; it is reported that about 100,000 have been thrown out of employment in the needlework industry alone. To those of us who live on the Atlantic seaboard, 25 cents an hour may seem far too small a wage, but its purchasing power may be adequate in a section of the country like Puerto Rico, where living costs are low. In any event, there is no absolute standard for wages, and where we fix one we run the danger of destroying the job.

Too rigid fixation of hours is similarly dangerous to employment. Hours have been steadily reduced in American industry, without legislation, and the 40-hour week is common. But in France it was decided to establish the 40-hour week by law—and that country has spent the past year trying to escape from the consequences. Industry after industry in France has been made exempt from the 40-hour limit because these industries were lagging far behind their normal productive capacity. When this happens, fewer men are employed—and it can hardly be comforting to those who lose their jobs to know that those who keep them work a shorter period of time.

The Social Security Act is another law that is in need of revision so that the humanitarian objectives of the Act may be realized without increasing the cost of employment. No one seems to deny that the enormous reserve fund which is being built up under the act is totally unnecessary; and this fund is collected by a tax on payrolls which it is particularly hard for the small business man to meet. There is now a 3 per cent tax on payrolls for unemployment insurance and a 1 per cent tax for old-age insurance. The latter tax will ultimately be increased to 3 per cent, so that the total federal tax will ultimately be 6 per cent. This means that every time an employer hires a man for, let us say, $100, he must pay $106 because of the tax. If he raises the wages of the worker, the tax is increased.*

As Benjamin Anderson, the economist of the Chase National Bank, has pointed out in a recent study of the subject, a tax on payrolls is a tax on employment. Confronted with artificially raised wage levels and with payroll taxes, at a time when profit margins are very small, American business is forced, against its best intentions and desires, to hold employment to a minimum and to reduce it, where possible, by substituting machinery. Now the use of machinery—what we call technological progress—is desirable where it is a logical step in producing things more cheaply and more easily. In that event the low-cost product made possible by the machine presumably finds a larger market, and more men are employed. Where the use of machinery is forced because of artificially raised costs of

---

* The employee also pays a tax of 1 per cent for old-age benefits, increasing to 3 per cent—which likewise tends to force the wage level up so that this tax will be absorbed by the employer.—W. L. W.

labor, however,—where it is merely used to maintain a situation without improving it,—there may be no such satisfactory result.

Of course, American wages are still not high enough. In a number of industries they are far less than profits would justify. But to attempt to raise them without reference to profits is simply to curtail the income of the worker by forcing an increase in unemployment. The American worker—like the investor and the business man—will profit when the profit-making possibilities of business are increased.

III

Because of our present tax program, we are not making full economic use of the earnings of individuals and corporations.

It is not the severity of American taxes which constitutes the principal danger of the tax legislation; it is the *kind of tax* that is imposed. An intelligent revision of taxes could probably produce the same revenue, while at the same time serving as a stimulus to free business enterprise.

Such a revision would be designed to encourage what is called "venture capital" — money invested not in bonds or savings accounts or gilt-edged securities, *but common stock money* that is willing to take the risk which new enterprises and expansions require, and which is the principal factor in creating new jobs.

The personal income tax is a perfectly logical and

reasonable method of collecting revenue—until it becomes so high that it drives capital out of industry and into tax-exempt securities. The first income tax was levied in 1913, and it proved so pleasant and easy for the tax collector that we have had a riot of state and federal income-tax laws since that time—without regard to the damage they might do to the nation's productive system.

The income tax isn't all: there is also the capital-gains tax. This ingenious device imposes a heavy tax on whatever profit a man makes out of a capital transaction; but if he happens to lose (and more men lose than win), he may deduct only a small portion of his losses from his income.

Now you may say that you are not very much concerned about the man who gets $10,000 in income and up: he can afford a high tax. And I say: all right, never mind what happens to him; but what happens to the country? Here is the type of man who ought to be providing our industries with venture capital. We need his money to finance the risks of new enterprises. But the capital-gains tax and the excessive income tax prevent us from using that money because it is put into tax-exempt securities or stays in the bank, where its investment is limited.

A very simple three-point program should remedy this situation: we should give the same weight to losses in the capital-gains tax as we give to gains; we should keep the tax on large incomes within productive limits; *and we should impose a tax on state and other govern-*

ment exempt securities. Indeed, if we are going to tax any investments, it would seem more reasonable to tax the safe ones and exempt those that are ventured for the sake of industry.

The tax on undistributed corporate profits, although it has been modified, is another tax that restricts investment. This is not quite as harmful as the discouragement of personal investment, because corporations cannot take risks as freely as an individual can take them; a corporation, being responsible to its security holders, has to be somewhat more careful. Nevertheless, one of the ways whereby a company expands is by ploughing back a part of its profits. It should be merely common sense to encourage this sort of thing if we are trying to find work for the ten million unemployed; but the tax law imposes a penalty on the corporation that builds a new plant out of earnings. The corporation must pay a tax on all profits not distributed in dividends—in addition to the corporation income tax. This may not be so hard on large corporations which have already built up their reserves, but it is a severe burden on a small corporation which can't save a dollar for itself without paying a tax on it.

An intelligent tax revision might be the most important economic achievement of our time.

IV

Because of the enormous discretionary power given to government bureaus and commissions, large and small businesses today are faced with the almost impossible task of operating under constantly changing rules.

Whenever a law is passed regulating an industry nowadays, a commission is set up to administer it. This means that the rules governing the industry are not fixed by Congress, but by the Commission; they may fluctuate with the Commission's personnel. Thus we have a highly personal form of government—a government of men, instead of a government of laws—in which the favor of a commission chairman determines the conduct of an industry that may be employing several hundred thousand people and be owned by several million stockholders.

For example, it is not the Securities Act which tells a corporation what it must do with respect to the sale of its securities, and it is not the Securities Exchange Act which tells the stock exchanges what they must do with respect to the securities traded in their markets. In both instances one must look, not primarily to the law, but to the Securities and Exchange Commission to find out what the requirements are. And it is not the Wagner Act which can guide a corporation in forming its industrial-relations program. It is the National Labor Relations Board. Likewise, no broadcasting station can read the law governing broadcasting and find out what rules it must observe. It has to consult with the Federal Communications Commission.

An industry can adapt itself to any reasonable law which sets out the requirements for that industry in black and white. But industry cannot successfully operate under a commission form of government, which may change its standards as it wills, and dispense its favors in accordance with the economic or social predilections of its members.

Even in the face of a "spend and spend, tax and tax" policy, the entrepreneur—always a hardy perennial—will continue to go ahead with his ideas on one condition—namely, that the rules are fixed and that he knows them in advance. In the course of a fairly active life—not all of it in the most dignified surroundings—I have played poker in odd corners of this continent with all kinds of people and under all conditions. It doesn't make any difference whether the ante is a penny or a dollar; and it doesn't make any difference what kind of clothes your companions in the game may wear or what language they may use, or even whether or not you might have difficulty at some later date in explaining how you happened to know them—you will play the game as long as the rules are fixed, and you will get out of the game just as soon as somebody starts changing them.

Even those who have been the principal promoters of this bureaucracy recognize these difficulties; but they say that the answer can be found in "the type of man you appoint." This is uncomfortably reminiscent of the "benevolent despotism" theory—namely, that a dictator isn't so bad as long as he is good. Aside from the basic unsoundness of this notion, we must realize that when we give a man such enormous power over industry we automatically incite in him the tendency to use it.

It is probably true that laws regulating modern industry are so complex that administrative commissions have become inevitable; but these commissions must rule, as Chief Justice Charles Evans Hughes recently stated, "with the recognized responsibility which attaches to judges and with the impartiality and independence which is associated with the judicial office."

In some instances the laws themselves require too much police work on the part of the commissioners. Because these laws were designed primarily as police measures—namely, to punish industry for past abuses and to forbid certain practices—it is time that they were reconsidered now, not in the light of what bad things they have prevented, but in the light of what good things they have contributed. It is not enough to say of a law that it has eliminated the evils of the nation's hard-bitten and speculative years. From this negative standpoint there is nothing so virtuous as a corpse. The question we need to ask is: has some of this restrictive legislation made industry "more dead than alive," or has it helped to revitalize industry and make it more useful?

The Securities Act and the Securities and Exchange Act, for example, have remedied certain abuses in the sale of securities to the public, and in the operation of the stock exchanges. That alone, however, does not justify this legislation. We shall want to know whether it has enabled the stock exchanges to perform

their job better.   Has it increased the liquidity of the
markets where the people must buy or sell their investments?   Has it aided the flow of private capital so
that industry may have the funds which it needs for expansion?

Unfortunately the unnecessary technical requirements of the Securities Acts have seriously restricted
the buying and selling of securities.   For this reason a
group of outstanding investment bankers and brokers
(spokesmen for seventeen stock exchanges represent-
ing the whole country) submitted a carefully-thought-
out proposal this spring for various amendments.   It
is disturbing to note that the report was lightly rejected
by the Chairman.* In a newspaper interview, William
O. Douglas stated: "Throwing things out so that the
boys in the Street can have another party isn't going
to help recovery."

The statement hardly seems to be relevant.   The objective in modifying the Exchange Act is not to give
the boys in the Street "another party."   The objective
is to provide industry with a life-giving flow of capital
*whether or not the boys in the Street incidentally en-
joy a party as a result*.   I emphasize the phrase because, to my mind, it is far better to accept a few
imperfections in a financial or industrial enterprise than
to create a condition of economic sterility in which vices
and virtues alike are dead.

Under the Public Utility Act of 1935 the utilities are

* William O. Douglas, then Chairman of the SEC, issued the official reply of the Commission on March 15, 1939.

now regulated by the Federal Power Commission and the Securities and Exchange Commission, in addition to the regulation already imposed upon them by the State Public Service Commissions. Unquestionably this mass of regulation has prevented the speculative errors of the pre-depression days; but it has also gone so far as to hamper efficient utility management and restrict the normal expansion of utility systems.

V

We do not need to rescind any of the laws regulating industry; but we need to amend them so as to encourage new enterprises which can absorb our idle money and our idle men. Business success is a far more hazardous speculation than most people realize. Even in the very active years between the World War and the depression, less than two thirds of the established American corporations made any money. Less than one third make any money today. These are established corporations. Among new business ventures, only one out of ten ever makes any money at all. Among the new industries developed since the war, there are three that have attracted considerable attention: the radio, the airplane, and air conditioning. All of these represented capital risks. They were ventures. They could not have developed at all unless men had been willing to take a chance. And it is interesting to note that only two or three companies in these industries have been able to pay any money on the common stock which represents the venture capital put into the enterprise.

A revision of the tax program so as to encourage investment; a reduction in government spending; a modification of the unnecessarily restrictive provisions of our economic legislation—these are the measures upon which business expansion waits. They are not easy measures to undertake—but they become easier as soon as they are undertaken. For example, a revision of the tax program should shortly increase the revenue from taxation; and the expansion of industry should shortly reduce the number who are living on government funds. We have accumulated a tremendous deficit of capital goods during the depression, and we shall need millions of men and billions of dollars to satisfy these needs.

Moreover, this program does not call upon us to sacrifice any of the moral gains of recent years. We do not have to get rid of the idea of "truth in securities." We do not have to abandon any plan for "social security" for the aged and the unemployed. We do not need to annul our provisions for collective bargaining, or reject the principle of federal supervision over industrial activities.

This is a campaign of revitalization which looks forward rather than back; which is not political in its nature, and should legitimately command the support of Republicans and Democrats, Conservatives and New Dealers, employers and employees. It is a program

for the assertion of one of our more neglected liberties
—that of free enterprise—with the same vigor as we
assert our liberties of speech, of press, and of religious
worship.

POLITICAL POWER:
THE TENNESSEE VALLEY
AUTHORITY

POLITICAL POWER:
THE TENNESSEE VALLEY
AUTHORITY

Reprinted from

THE ATLANTIC MONTHLY

of August, 1937.

During the five-year struggle between the Tennessee Valley Authority and the Commonwealth and Southern Corporation, of which Mr. Willkie was President, Mr. Willkie published a number of articles in which he presented his case to the public. This article has been selected as a typical presentation of his point of view on the Utility question.

POLITICAL POWER:
THE TENNESSEE VALLEY
AUTHORITY

By Wendell Willkie

I

PROLONGED controversy on any subject is apt to engender such bitterness that fair and dispassionate consideration becomes extremely difficult. This is a truth that husbands and wives know well. On a larger panorama, history has frequently demonstrated it—as witness such random examples as the slave issue in 1860, the war debts in 1931, the responsibility of "Wall Street" in the late depression. In their respective periods these important topics were discussed in a highly emotional atmosphere, and solutions found in such situations are apt to be more violent than thoughtful, more punitive than sane.

For nearly a decade now, the forum for the discussion of electric power has had the appearance of a battlefield, with the militant reformers, the public-ownership advocates, and the politicians engaging in a no-quarter combat with the utilities. Incidentally, one of the first guns fired was an article by Professor William Z. Ripley, entitled "More Light!—And Power Too," in the *Atlantic* for November 1926.

This was a vigorous exposé of the elaborate pyramids which certain financial promoters in the industry had built up for their own profit.   It started a series of more or less violent criticisms of the industry, including a long seven-year investigation made and effectively publicized by the Federal Trade Commission.

By 1933 it was clear that the Administration was prepared to take drastic action against the utility industry.   Upon his accession to office, President Roosevelt denounced the utilities in no uncertain terms.   The Tennessee Valley Authority Act, putting the government in competition with private power companies, was passed in 1933.   The Public Utility Act, containing the famous death sentence on utility holding companies and severely regulating all interstate utilities, was passed in the fall of 1935.

Today there are not only forty-three state commissions regulating the public utilities within state borders; there are also fourteen Federal agencies concerned with power.   Of these, the two most important *regulating* agencies are the Federal Power Commission, principally concerned with utility operations, and the Securities and Exchange Commission, principally concerned with utility holding companies and utility financing.

But that is not all.   Several of these agencies—notably the Tennessee Valley Authority—represent government projects which are engaged, or will engage, in the generation and sale of electric power. These agencies are free from restriction and regulation by state or Federal commissions. Thus the utility industry, bound by a network of regulation, must compete with the government as an unregulated competitor of extraordinary wealth and power.

II

Through the Tennessee Valley Authority the government is launching its power program principally in the five states of Tennessee, North Carolina, Georgia, Alabama, and Mississippi. Since the government has already constructed Boulder Dam on the Colorado River, and is constructing Bonneville and Grand Coulee on the Columbia, and since the President has asked for seven more regional authorities similar to the TVA, presumably the government will extend its campaign to cover the nation.

Like England's once famous military formation, the British Square, the TVA has had four fronts to present to the public, and it uses the front most suitable to the group which it is addressing. Before the courts it claims that it is not really a power enterprise, but primarily a *conservation* activity: it is a project to prevent floods, promote navigation on the Tennessee River, and check soil erosion in the great Tennessee Valley. Only before a more sympathetic audience is it frankly an instrument for the electrification of America.

This quadruple picture of the TVA has undoubtedly

been helpful to it. The American people have been stirred by stories of what is happening to the soil in the great agricultural areas in the Middle West. Many thousands have seen the huge TVA dams with the water banked impressively behind them, and have seen green life returning to soil that was previously bleak and pitted. They have been told about the plans to make the river navigable, about the plans to prevent floods. They have naturally been as enthusiastic about these objectives as about the general idea of "cheap power."

The TVA has therefore appeared to be on the side of the angels in the controversy between it and the utilities. But the conservation program of the TVA is only a masquerade. It has no functional connection with the power program of the Authority, and the amount spent on it is only an insignificant portion of the Authority's total expenditures. Other departments of government, both state and national, are charged with the duty of caring for soil erosion and are doing such work effectively without the building of dams and power facilities. The TVA dams are obviously useless for soil erosion. And if they were really designed for navigation and flood control, then the government has seldom engaged in a more wasteful and less effective operation. The TVA plan calls for constructing eleven dams at a present estimate of $520,-600,000. On the basis of such information as has been given in committee hearings, it appears that about

$190,000,000 of this will be allocated to power facilities. The difference—$330,600,000—is apparently for navigation and flood control.

But the Army engineers had reported (House Document 328, March 4, 1930) that for the purposes of navigation low-head dams could have been built on the river, with the same size and depth of locks, at a cost of $74,709,000. This would leave a remainder of $255,891,000 for flood control. The engineers also estimated that the average annual loss from floods on the Tennessee River was about $981,000. Thus the expenditure for flood control would be about 250 times the average annual loss from floods.

These conclusions have been quite disturbing to the Directors of the TVA. In testimony before committees of Congress, they have questioned the conclusions of the Army engineering corps, which is considered by many the ablest engineering group in the country and particularly expert on the subject of inland waterways.

Obviously, also, flood control could not have been the principal purpose of the TVA, since a flood-control system would call for empty reservoirs having no power value, while the apparent plan is to fill a portion of the reservoirs at certain times of the year, although damaging floods may occur in any month of the year. These obvious facts were recognized when the Miami, Ohio, Conservancy flood-control dams were built by Dr. Arthur E. Morgan. There is a large plaque on these dams which reads:

THE DAMS
OF THE MIAMI CONSERVATORY DISTRICT ARE FOR
FLOOD PREVENTION PURPOSES
THEIR USE FOR POWER DEVELOPMENT
OR FOR STORAGE
WOULD BE A MENACE TO
THE CITIES BELOW

Outside of the courtroom, the advocates of the TVA
have been less guarded in their statements. Mr.
David E. Lilienthal in an address at Knoxville, Tennessee, on March 1, 1935, said:—

But there seems to be some inclination to forget that these
dams are not being built for scenic effect. These millions of
dollars are not being spent merely to increase business activity
in this area. These dams are power dams. They are being built
because they will produce electric power.

And it seems likely that no one of the three Directors
would today deny that the generation and sale of power
constitute a major function, if not *the* major function
of the Tennessee Valley Authority.

Indeed, although the TVA is only at the beginning of
its power operations, these already represent a considerable enterprise. At the present time the TVA
transmission lines extend for 1300 miles and parallel
and criss-cross the line of the private companies. They
reach out into many of the principal markets. They are
already serving 17 municipalities, 13 coöperatives,
with 30,000 individual customers. The TVA program
contemplates the building of eleven hydro plants.
Three of these are completed, two more will be com-

pleted in 1939, and all by 1942. They will produce
5,780,000,000 kilowatt-hours per year, which is about
one half the total present production of all the power
facilities in the seven states in the Tennessee Valley.*

The American people, therefore, are paying more
than half a billion dollars for eleven dams, chiefly designed to supply power to one area. But this power,
as will shortly be demonstrated, is to be supplied to this
area at *less than cost*. In other words, the TVA will
operate annually at a deficit, and these annual deficits
must, of course, be paid for out of the pockets of the
taxpayers.

III

The sponsors of the TVA maintained at the beginning that this vast program was not designed to create
a competitive power system, but to set up a yardstick
by which the rates of the private companies could be
judged. The yardstick idea was undoubtedly attrac-
tive, since, after all, the average consumer did not understand much about electric rates and had no way of
personally checking their relative highness or lowness.

Unfortunately, the yardstick is rubber from the first
inch to the last.

From the generation of power at the beginning to its
distribution to the ultimate consumer at the end, the
TVA enjoys privileges and exemptions which are denied to the private utility, which conceal the true cost
of TVA power, and the cost of which comes out of the

* As of August, 1937.

pockets of you and me as taxpayers. These can be best illustrated by a direct comparison between the TVA and the Tennessee Electric Power Company, one of the typical companies in the Commonwealth and Southern System operating in that area.

The first advantage given to the TVA is exemption from practically all taxes. For the fiscal year ended June 30, 1936, the TVA paid only $45,347 in taxes. The Tennessee Electric Power Company (with approximately the same capital investment) paid $2,339,284 in taxes. Here is a difference in this item alone of $2,293,937.

Let us turn to the item of depreciation. This is an expense, a cost of operation, just as much as labor and fuel. This cost to the Tennessee Company, fixed and determined by the Tennessee Railroad and Public Utilities Commission, amounts to $1,260,000 per year. The books of the TVA, however, carry no item for depreciation.

The same is true with respect to interest charges. The Tennessee Company properties were built only in part with borrowed capital. During the twelve months ended June 30, 1936, this company paid interest and preferred dividends amounting to $4,299,022. On the other hand, the property of the TVA is built entirely with borrowed capital. The United States Government is paying interest and will continue to pay interest on such borrowings. The TVA books, however, show no item to cover this interest. It got its property from the Federal Government, which in turn, of course, collected its money from the taxpayer.

With our comparison limited to the items of taxes, depreciation, and interest charges, the yardstick fails to be a fair comparison for the Tennessee Company by $7,852,959 per year. This is twice the amount which the residential customers pay the company annually for all the electricity they use. It is 65 per cent of the entire electric sales of the company, including sales to power users and street lighting. Or, to put it in another way, the Tennessee Company, if given the same "special arbitrary advantages" given the TVA, could sell electricity at rates much lower than those the TVA has set up as the yardstick.

But these constitute only part of the subsidies. They have to do only with the operation of the TVA system, largely devoted to generation of the power at the plant and with transmission up to the point of distribution. It is the objective of the TVA to sell its power to municipalities and to get these municipalities to erect their own distribution systems. For this purpose the municipalities can obtain an outright grant of funds to an amount of 30 per cent to 45 per cent of the cost of the system. They can borrow the balance from the United States Government at a low rate of interest.

Curiously enough, the method by which the TVA pursues its ends—namely, duplication of facilities—has been condemned by all students of the power program on whatever side of the line they may belong. Mr. David Lilienthal, one of the Directors of the

TVA, has frankly acknowledged this method, stating, "The Authority is under duty to acquire a market for its power. It is authorized to compete with existing utilities, and for this purpose is expressly empowered to erect duplicate facilities."

But, with few exceptions, public-ownership men and utility executives both agree that duplication of a private system by a government power system is directly contrary to public interest and means higher rates paid by the consumer and higher taxes by the taxpayer. So generally accepted is this opinion that it should be necessary to quote only from Mr. J. D. Ross,* recently appointed by President Roosevelt to the Securities and Exchange Commission, and for some time superintendent of the municipal power plant in Seattle, Washington. In his report for 1935, Mr. Ross stated that as a result of competition between the city power plant and a private company, "the cost of distribution, which is far the larger part of the total cost to serve, is doubled, while the revenue is cut in two. The customer must, in the end, pay the cost."

Since the TVA is apparently selling its power at less than cost, it should say so. If people who live in New York City, for example, are to pay part of the electric bill of people who live in Corinth, Mississippi, the people in New York should know about it. Perhaps they will not object. On more than one occasion the American people as a whole have contributed, through taxes, to a development designed to serve only a limited

* Mr. Ross died March 14, 1939.

area. Often that is socially desirable. But if we are to pay part of the electric light bills of the Tennessee Valley, the TVA should honestly tell us so.

Also, if the TVA is attempting to force the utilities into public ownership, it should employ means that will neither deceive nor injure the public and will not jeopardize the interests of utility investors. It should announce its intention and proceed, by condemnation proceedings duly instituted in the courts of the land, to take over utility properties with fair compensation to the owners. This is both the honest and the humane method of action. Also, it gives the people a fair chance to protest if they don't like the change; or if they are still skeptical of political management of a major industry; or if they are a little worried about adding to the national debt the twelve billion dollars necessary to replace the present private investment in the industry.

IV

As can be imagined, the utility companies operating in the Tennessee Valley have been helpless to meet the subsidized government competition which the TVA has presented. The first immediate effect is seen in their inability to finance their capital requirements.

The problem of financing is a particularly serious matter for a utility company, because of two peculiar characteristics of the business. First, the utility company is required by law to supply service to anyone who applies for it. Second, it is limited by law in the rates it can charge and, therefore, in the amount of revenue it can receive. These two characteristics mean that a utility company cannot finance itself out of revenue— as the Ford Company has done with such conspicuous success, and as all great corporations are able to do in part. Also, it can never say, as other companies might say: "We have grown large enough and we shall produce now for a limited market."

In the utility business the property is continually expanding. It expands every time a new customer puts in his order. Whenever a utility man goes to his office, he knows that he will face a need that day for additional capital to meet new requirements for electric service.

Out of every dollar of revenue received by Commonwealth and Southern companies in the Southeast, they expend approximately 26½ cents for labor, 13½ cents for taxes, 39½ cents for borrowed capital, and 20½ cents for materials and supplies. Obviously, these companies should not reduce the wages they pay. They cannot reduce the taxes. They cannot control the present high costs of material and supplies. The only real economy they can achieve is to reduce the cost of capital. The competition of the TVA barred the utilities in that area from borrowing in the money market at the recent favorable rates—even though they had the same normal increase in business during the last three years that utilities elsewhere have had. If these Southeastern companies could have refunded their senior securities on the same basis as that followed in 1936 by the Northern companies in the same system, they could have saved six million dollars a year in interest and preferred dividends. This is equal to 40 per cent of the entire amount they receive annually from their more than 430,000 domestic electric consumers in the South.

The utilities were therefore blocked from their principal opportunity to economize—namely, reduction of fixed charges. They have seen their customers taken away from them, the value of their property seriously impaired, and the interests of their stockholders unfairly injured. Against this they had only one immediate weapon—and that was the law. The utilities took to the courts. The companies in the Commonwealth and Southern System, of which I am president, were active among the nineteen operating utilities which sought an injunction against the TVA efforts to duplicate their lines and take away their markets.

We have been severely criticized for this, but I have no apology for it and believe that none is needed. It seems to me that responsible company executives had no other choice than to seek to preserve the property of their stockholders through every possible legal means. Various decisions have been rendered by the lower courts on the Tennessee Valley Authority Act, but since the cases have not yet reached the United States Supreme Court,* the constitutionality of the act

* On January 30, 1939, the Supreme Court handed down a 5-2 decision without deciding the constitutional issue, saying that all the private companies which challenged the Government's power program

has still to be determined.   This delay has certainly not been the fault of the utilities, which have been more than anxious to have the issue settled.* As Arthur Krock stated recently in the *New York Times*:

> Such delay as there has been in getting a forthright decision on general TVA power policy appears to be the fault of the government, which for months dodged a submission of the clear issue and has only recently shown interest in getting one.

As I have stated, I believe that the utility companies would have been neglecting their duty if they had failed to resort to the courts to protect their property.   But I am under no delusion as to the value of litigation. Courts merely answer questions, but do not solve problems.   The fundamental problem in this case is whether or not public ownership of the light and power industry is desirable.

V

As a rule the leaders in this government power program have avoided the phrase, "public ownership," which still has a harsh ring in many American ears. Occasionally, however, they have frankly indicated that this is the program's objective.   Clearly, that must be its result.   Nor will it be helpful for business men to regard such a result instinctively with horror.   It is

---

had "no right to be free of competition" and "no standing to maintain the suit."

*In the so-called Ashwander Case, the Supreme Court merely decided that the generation and transmission of power from Wilson Dam was constitutional, but expressly refrained from giving any opinion as to the constitutionality of the act as a whole.—W. L. W.

just another way—to my mind, an inferior way—of doing the job.

But there is nothing sacred about private operation of business. The utilities have no God-given charter for existing. Provided that the government compensates for what it destroys (a provision which, unfortunately, we cannot take for granted), there is no reason why the government should not put the utility companies out of business if the people want the government to do so. The only question which the people are interested in—and this is the issue which bitterness has obscured—is: *What is the best way to generate and distribute electric power efficiently and economically?*

Amid the claims and counter-claims, amid the rabble-rousing on both sides, amid the efforts to hide the government's power activities, amid the benign references to "soil reclamation, navigation, and flood control," let us keep an eye fixed upon this objective. It is of particular importance because electric power in a few years will be far more indispensable to our manner of living than now.

And it is important to us *now* because we are now determining the policy that shall govern this power in the future. We must make up our minds very quickly as to who shall own and operate our electric power systems—or else we shall wake up some morning in the not distant future and find that the decision has been made for us. It will then be too late to change—at least without great difficulty. The time to decide on the design for a house is before it is built.

Before the government stepped belligerently into the rôle of protector of the people against the power companies, the utility industry had accomplished a rather extraordinary job in America. Interruptions in power service in any community are very rare today, and it is significant that, amid the avalanche of criticism poured on the industry, few have had any complaints against its operating efficiency. Between 1913 and 1936, rates in the industry declined 46 per cent, while the cost of living, in general, increased about the same amount. Some 22,000,000 families and farms in America now have electric power at their service at an average cost of about $34 per year, or a little more than 9 cents a day.

Certainly no one would deny that the job cannot be further improved. Utility men, when they are sure no one will overhear them, will occasionally admit that the punitive legislation by the government has spurred them to renewed efforts to lower their rates and put their houses in order. Of course the State Public Service Commissions are supposed to keep a vigilant eye upon the utilities for just that purpose, but the glance of the Federal eye has augmented this optical influence.

Under public ownership, however, there is no one in authority to see that electric service is efficiently handled, or to see that the voter is not deceived into thinking that his rates are low, when in reality he is paying for his electricity indirectly out of taxes. The weakness of government ownership was defined for all time in the statement made by Thomas Edison, as follows:—

There is far more danger in public monopoly than there is in private monopoly, for when the government goes into business it can always shift its losses to the taxpayers. If it goes into the power business, it can pretend to sell cheap power and then cover up its losses. The government never really goes into business, for it never makes ends meet, and that is the first requisite of business. It just mixes a little business with a lot of politics, and no one ever gets a chance to find out what is actually going on.

VI

In countries at all comparable to the United States the record of public ownership is not impressive. Of course, Sweden is frequently cited as an example of what public ownership can do in the light and power industry, but the comparison is of little value because the objects compared are so dissimilar. Sweden is a small, compact, homogeneous country, simple in political, social, and industrial structure. In size it would fit along this country's Atlantic Seaboard.

There are no large countries in which government ownership has finally demonstrated its efficiency on a large scale. Within the United States, government operation of the railroads during the World War was obviously a fiasco from which the railroads have recovered only after years of effort. That may not be a fair illustration, however, since it took place in a war period, and had to be handled as an emergency matter.

We have at hand a more apt exhibit in the Postal System, a government enterprise which is usually regarded with approval by public-ownership advocates.

As these last frequently point out, the mail in this country is delivered with reasonable promptness and reliability. Unfortunately for this record, however, the Post Office has been operated at a very considerable deficit ever since it was organized. Complete figures on the costs of the Post Office would have to be tracked down through a maze of government reports of all kinds, both legislative and executive; such figures are not given in the reports of the Post Office Department. But the 1936 report of the Department states that the *operating* deficit of the United States Post Office in the past one hundred years amounts to $1,601,569,000.

That is simply the *operating* deficit. It does not include the enormous amounts of money spent on the capital investment in post offices—namely, the money spent for the purchase of land and for the construction of post-office buildings. These were all taken out of other appropriations and were, therefore, not charged against the Post Office Department—which is one of the ways whereby a government department achieves an apparent cost reduction. There were 13,730 post offices and 1501 classified stations and branches on June 30, 1936. There are no figures for the capital expenditures herein represented, but the total must be enormous and the fixed charges thereon would have to be added to the operating deficit mentioned above.

If a corporation similar to the American Telephone and Telegraph Company should take over the administration of the Post Office, it is my belief that we should have an even more efficient mail service, at present rates, without any deficit at all. It is more than likely that the rates could be reduced. That, of course, is merely a personal opinion which cannot be proved. But the illustration gives rise to this very important question: Would we consider it to be efficient operation if the government were to run the light and power industry as it runs the Post Office?

Let us remember that the Postal System is still the chief source of political patronage, and that postal officers have long been appointed on the basis of their party affiliations—despite the fact that every President within my memory has advocated that the merit system should be adopted. Aside from that, however, a business which operates at a loss—a loss which in the end must be paid by the taxpayer—is not a business that is efficiently and economically run. We may well ask ourselves the question, in considering public ownership, whether the power industry should be run in a business-like fashion or whether it should definitely be a Federal charity.

VII

If we decide that in view of these facts we do not want public ownership, what alternative is there to the present TVA program? Three of the great dams have already been completed at enormous cost. Obviously we cannot tear them down, nor should we let this investment stay entirely idle. What constructive solution can the utilities offer which would save not only the nation's investment in these government properties, but also the people's investment in the utility industry? At the same time, what solution would best serve that objective which we laid down in this article as the real purpose of any power program—namely, *the most economical and efficient generation and distribution of power*?

Beginning with 1935, the utilities have made several proposals, but to date they have all been either disregarded or rejected by the government. It was suggested, first, that if the TVA was to be an honest yardstick it should observe the same requirements as those imposed upon the private utilities. In other words, it should pay taxes at the same rate, keep uniform accounts, charge rates so as to produce a fair return, and file its rates with the State Commissions and the Federal Power Commission. This would seem to be a reasonable suggestion, but it did not meet with the approval of the TVA authorities.

In subsequent interviews with TVA and other governmental officials, the Commonwealth and Southern group of companies has made further suggestions, which can be summarized as follows:—

1. To purchase the power produced in the government plants and redistribute it at rates fixed by the Federal Power Commission.

2. To sell to the TVA all our systems in that territory at a

price to be fixed either by negotiation or by condemnation proceedings in a court.

3. To enter into a pooling arrangement whereby both government and utilities would pool their power facilities, and these
would be used on the most economical basis to fill public or private requirements.

So far not only have all the proposals been rejected,
but no substitute proposal has been forthcoming from
the other side. Last January, Dr. Arthur E. Morgan,
head of the TVA, made a public statement which—although I disagreed with certain parts of it—was so fair
in its approach that we hoped a solution was near at
hand. While Dr. Morgan is in favor of public ownership, he expressed his belief that the transition should
be gradual and only undertaken in so far as experience
justifies it. At the same time, he believed that duplication of facilities should be avoided, that public-ownership reports should be factual, and that government
yardsticks should be honest. Deploring the bitterness
of feeling between utilities and government power
spokesmen, he uttered a plea for coöperation rather
than violence, warning that "the manner in which we
achieve our ends may have a more enduring influence
on the country than the ends we may achieve."

The utility industry is naturally opposed to public
ownership, but it cannot quarrel with so reasonable an
approach to the question. Unfortunately, no echo of
Dr. Morgan's statement has been heard in other government quarters. Official tongues still lash the utilities and recommend no compromise. The President

has discontinued his power conference. The TVA is vigorously expanding its competitive power activities. Seven other TVA's are in process of preparation. As the utilities read the signs, the energies of the government seem to be dedicated to battle rather than peaceful negotiation.

But if that reading is correct, then it is surely the duty of a sovereign government to announce its intentions. The utilities have a right to know, officially and not by guess, exactly what the government plans to do with them. That includes their quarter of a million employees and their four or five million investors. And the American people have the right to consider these plans in advance and to determine whether or not their execution is desirable.

AN INTERVIEW ON TVA

On June 14, 1940, an interview with Wendell Willkie by George Carmack, Editor of the Knoxville "News-Sentinel", was published in the Scripps-Howard newspapers. It is reprinted here as a footnote to Mr. Willkie's earlier article on the TVA, since it indicates his present attitude.

Wendell L. Willkie today expressed an opinion "that you can't turn the clock back on TVA." Mr. Willkie, president of the Commonwealth & Southern Corporation, which locked horns spectacularly with the Ten-

nessee Valley Authority, declared than any attempt to
force TVA to "retrogress" would be futile.

"Any President of the United States who tried to
turn TVA back to the private utilities would be extremely unrealistic," he asserted in an interview for the
Scripps-Howard newspapers.

HAVE A QUARREL

"To say that I have no quarrel with the way TVA
was established and was operated during its period of
expansion would be dishonest," Mr. Willkie said.

"I will say that its establishment in the Tennessee
Valley was ruthless. But there it is; these dams have
been built, distribution systems have been acquired. It
is an accomplished fact. Now let's give TVA a real
and honest chance to see what it can do or cannot do
for the benefit of all the people."

Mr. Willkie does not believe that TVA should expand to take in more territory. But he believes that in
its present territory it should not be "unfairly dis-
turbed."

"There is one thing I do demand of TVA," he said,
"I think TVA itself should demand it. That is an honest, fair, crystal-clear system of bookkeeping that will
let the people know exactly what TVA is doing, and
what its efficiency is in comparison with the private
utilities.

"Let's not only show its cost but clearly show the
differential of cost between its operation and that of a

private company. Let's see it operate in this territory over a long enough period to give it a real test—say five years. Then the people will be able to decide whether it should be expanded, contracted or just what. Such procedure is the democratic process.

"I think some method should be set up to take care of expansion, if expansion ever should be voted on. Back in 1934 that was my greatest criticism of TVA.

"I went to Mr. Roosevelt in 1934, and to the TVA Board, and offered to sell the Tennessee Electric Power properties that TVA later acquired. The offer was refused. Five years of wrangling, five years of letting water which is power flow unused down the Tennessee River, followed. Then in 1939 we sold these properties to TVA for $80,000,000, not far from the figure we would have sold for in 1934.

"I think some impartial board should have been set up—I think it still should be set up, if after a real test of TVA an expansion of the system is decided on—to set a fair price on properties taken over.

"I don't think TVA should be both judge and advocate."

Soil Conservation Praised

One phase of TVA's program which won unstinted praise from Mr. Willkie is its soil-conservation program.

"That has been a job well done," he said. "The program should be continued and, if anything, enlarged.

Soil conservation is a very proper governmental function."

He believes TVA should be run in the manner of a private corporation.

"TVA should be allowed to choose its employees as does a corporation," he said. "Political patronage must be kept out. Its personnel must be chosen and advanced on a merit basis.

"I have never heard any criticism of TVA's choice of employees and I don't think political patronage has got into the system. I see no reason for changing the present set up as far as employee selection and management are concerned."

Mr. Willkie said he thought TVA should pay taxes in just the same manner and same proportion as the private utilities. "But if this isn't done, in its bookkeeping and its reports to the public this difference in tax burden should be made clear to the public."

SUGGESTION ON INCOME

Subject to reasonable restrictions by Congress, he believes TVA should be allowed to handle its income much as the income of a private corporation is handled.

TVA has three dams under construction, the final three of its original program of 10 dams. Mr. Willkie would not commit himself specifically as to the completion of these dams, but he did say that they should be completed if TVA's financial operation and the state of the "public purse" permitted.

"The public debt is reaching toward the staggering figure of $45,000,000,000," he said. "Then to top it off we're going to spend upwards of 10 billions for defense.

ALL MUST PAY

"I think we are going to enter into a period of economy outside the field of defense. That is very understandable, because the taxes are going to hit enough people so that it hurts.

"Already the base is being broadened with lower exemptions and rates are being upped in fairly low brackets. That is necessary. It can't all come from the rich, because if we took all their income it still wouldn't be enough to pay the bills.

"This tax spread is going to make all the country economy-conscious. TVA's appropriations may be affected."

However, Mr. Willkie did have this to say concerning the dams:

"Nothing is more important than defense, and there is nothing which might well mask more political logrolling than the flag-waving variety of national defense.

WOULD ACT ON ARMY'S ADVICE

"But if some impartial group, the United States Army or its engineers for instance, did say that the completion of these dams was a link in our national defense, the dams should be completed and as rapidly as those charged with our defense thought necessary and possible."

Mr. Willkie was outspoken in favor of rural electrification, which he said he considered not an economic but a social problem.

"I proposed a plan to the President a long time ago, under which a revolving fund of $100,000,000 would be set up to take care of rural electrification," he said.

WOULD MAKE UP LOSSES

"Take this power into the farm homes, and then make up—either to TVA, if in its area, or to the private power companies if in their areas—the loss that carrying power to these rural areas would entail. As the load builds up, these areas might well become profitable. When they do, let the original government expenditure be paid back out of profits and used to replenish the revolving funds."

Mr. Willkie pulled no punches in his criticism of certain TVA methods. But he did express a belief that the period of agitation over public vs. private utilities was a thing of the past until TVA's program has a chance to prove its merit or lack of merit.

AN ADDRESS AT THE
UNIVERSITY OF INDIANA
ON FOUNDATION DAY

AN ADDRESS AT THE
UNIVERSITY OF INDIANA
ON FOUNDATION DAY

*Delivered at the University, Bloomington,
Indiana, on May 4th, 1938.*

AN ADDRESS AT THE
UNIVERSITY OF INDIANA
ON FOUNDATION DAY

By *Wendell Willkie*

ACCORDING to custom, those who are invited to attend the celebrations of a university are usually men or women who have attained eminence in scholarship. I come to you today with no such distinction. I did, indeed, graduate from Indiana, but I am afraid that much of what I learned here I have forgotten, and since those days my life has been spent in the market place, entirely remote from academic cloisters.

The question may well arise, therefore, as to why I am here at all. I am certainly not here because I like to speak. And I am certainly not here because I think you like to hear me speak. Frankly, the real reason I come back is because I haven't been back to an academic function since I graduated twenty-five years ago, and I have now a very keen interest in finding out what has been happening on this campus in the past twenty-five years.

In the world at large, a great deal has happened during this period. In fact, I don't believe you could find another quarter-century in history so packed with momentous events in the life of mankind. For example, we have lived through a world war in this twenty-five year period. We have lived through one major depression and two minor ones. We have seen the governments of at least half the people in the world drastically altered in character. We have witnessed the development of half a dozen big industries, several of which—the automobile, the radio and the airplane—have had a major effect on the way we live. We have seen the social customs of a hundred years' standing rejected by a generation that wanted to make its own rules.

On the basis of these considerations, you may be expecting me to say that at the end of these twenty-five years I find the world very greatly changed. As a matter of fact, although there has been considerable rearrangement of men, methods and masters, fundamentally I don't think we have changed very much. Whether for good or for ill, the principles by which men live remain the same as when I sat where you are sitting and heard someone tell me that my classmates and I were the hope of the world.

As one gets older, one becomes a little skeptical about the quick reforms that are designed to create the perfect state in a short period of time. We are continually tempted by catchwords to think of nations standing at the crossroads, with their fate depending on which road they choose. But the destiny of mankind is neither as simple nor as fragile as that. I cannot

tell you how many "new worlds" we have been building in these twenty-five years, for example, nor have I
time to enumerate the many "grave crises" the world
has managed to survive.   Any man who has lived
through this quarter-century is apt to develop a certain
immunity, like that of the adult world toward measles,
to the crises, cataclysms and catastrophes which we are
called upon to face every year.

The last war, of course, was "the greatest in history," and so was the depression, and so was the boom
period.   A dozen times, I am sure, we were warned of
"a great moral breakdown in the character of our people," and a revolution to be led by one group or
another has been at our doors off and on many times.
According to commentators both here and abroad, we
have witnessed "the collapse of democracy," just about
as often as we have witnessed "the downfall of the cap-
italist system."   New Deals and New Freedoms, Red
perils and the iron hand of militarism have confronted
us day in and day out, and we have managed to
carry on.

One of the things you will learn in your careers is
that the world has a habit of emerging from soul-
shattering conflicts with its soul still unshattered.   I
suspect that the campus of this University has maintained a similar basic immutability amid the excite-
ments of the past twenty-five years.   Frankly, I don't
expect it to be very different, and I don't expect that
you are any more heroic or less heroic than the young
men and women who sat here twenty-five years ago.

In other words, I don't think you are a lost generation any more than you are a saved one. I don't think the world will stand or fall depending upon what your decisions in life may be. The world is a pretty tough organization, and even if this year's graduates from the University of Indiana should embark on careers of assault and battery, the world would, I think, be able to shake off your depredations without any very great harm. Similarly, if every one of you should carry a sword as fearless and honorable as Galahad's, I doubt if the world would thereupon enter the millennium.

If I should make a careful inspection of the University, therefore, after this lapse of twenty-five years, I should undoubtedly find, in addition to the new buildings, some new maps in the geographies, some new chapters in the histories, some new courses never heard of in my time, some new activities on the campus, some new customs. But I should be very much surprised if I found that your outlook on the world that lay outside these things was very different from mine. Even if I happen to have lost touch with the substance of the University, I do not think I have lost touch with its spirit.

I am aware that the phrase, "the spirit of an institution," is a vague one, and I should like to define what I mean by it. I would say that the outstanding characteristic of the spirit of Indiana was—and, I think, still is—its liberalism.

We have heard a great deal about liberalism in recent years, which is a pretty good sign that the peo-

ple are a little concerned about it. Just as we don't
talk much about bread and water unless we foresee a
scarcity, so we are apt to take liberalism for granted
until it shows signs of disappearing. In Europe several of the major countries have very frankly decided
that liberalism isn't worth it. And even in America
we have bandied the word about rather loosely until it
has lost some of its meaning and has vague political
implications.

Of course, liberalism is not the property of any one
political party nor the product of any one political
platform. It is not a fixed program of action nor a
vote on this or that particular measure. *Liberalism is
an attitude of mind.* The liberal, for example, might
be opposed to regulation of business in one instance and
in favor of it in another. The criterion of the liberal
philosophy is this: in the faith of the liberal the emphasis is upon individual freedom, while in the ideolo-
gies of either the Right or Left it is upon social control.

You can make out quite a case for social control.
Mussolini and Hitler have apparently convinced their
people that it is desirable. You can say that a democracy which permits too much individual freedom moves
too slowly. There are a number of people who are
willing to sacrifice their freedom for the sake of what
they believe will be greater efficiency and prosperity.
Personally, I am convinced that there is no possibility
for continuing prosperity for the great mass of people except in a free political society and under a free,

if supervised, economy. Perhaps this is wrong, but even so, in the words of Newton Baker, "there are still many who would prefer to be poor, if necessary, but, in any case, free."

The liberal movement therefore strikes at the forces of autocracy whether they bear the label of business or government or society. It may thus be opposed to a business program at one time, and to a government program at another. And nothing illustrates this more effectively than the parallel between the liberal movement when I was your age and the true liberal movement today.

Those of you who are undergraduates will not recall the liberal movement of the first fifteen years of this century, which was in full tide at the time I was in college. I can assure you, however, that the cause was an exciting one. As undergraduates we were certainly as much interested in it as you may be interested in current political and economic trends.

The early twentieth century represented the period in which the great industrial organizations reached their fullest development and influence. Gigantic combines had been built in Banking, in Oil, in Tobacco, in Steel, in Meat Packing and in other industries. In particular, the Railroads, which by that time covered the continent, were the representatives of enormous financial power.

In the development of many of these industries political influence had played an important part. The big corporation worked through political bosses in obtain-

ing favorable government decisions. To a degree
which we have never witnessed since, American business not only participated in the people's government,
but frequently played a dominant part therein.

By their political power the industries of the East
were able to get the franchises they wanted, to establish
monopolies, to control legislation, to fatten themselves
on high tariffs at the expense of the agricultural West
and the South.

It is not surprising that the American people began
to resent this corporate supremacy over government.
The leading liberal publications denounced the vested
corporate interests that were in control of American
politics. The leading figures in national affairs began
to demand freedom for the average man against big
business and high finance. And the average man himself, in increasing numbers, began to think that that
was a good idea.

For its leadership this movement was fortunate in
getting three of the greatest of Americans—all three
men of very different backgrounds, inclinations and
talents—Theodore Roosevelt, Robert La Follette and
Woodrow Wilson. I think we should also include in
the list of those who inspired the pre-war liberal movement the name of a man from Indiana—Senator Albert
J. Beveridge, who gave the keynote speech at the National Convention of the Progressive Party in 1912,
calling for "a representative government that represents the people," and urging his party to "battle for
the actual rights of man."

Well, there is no time here to go into that long and colorful campaign which led to anti-trust prosecutions, to new legislation, to the quarrel between Roosevelt and Taft, to the split between Republicans and Progressives, to the election of Woodrow Wilson, and then came to an end with the world war.

The objectives of the movement were largely achieved. The oil trust, the tobacco trust, the beef trust and the other monopolies were dissolved. What Wilson called "the money trust" was ended by the Federal Reserve Act in 1913. The great corporate hand of the monopolies was pushed out of the State and Federal Legislatures, and the effort to re-establish popular control led to the direct election of Senators, the giving of votes to women, and the enactment of income-tax legislation on the principle of adjusting the tax to the ability to pay. By 1914, in his message to Congress, Woodrow Wilson was able to state: "Our program of legislation with respect to business is now virtually complete. * * * The road at last lies clear and firm before business."

That, briefly, was the cause that enlisted the enthusiasm of the liberals of my time—the cause of the people against corporate domination. Perhaps if there had not been a war, the road would have remained clear for business. But the war gave to business all over the world the highly artificial character of a war activity, and the governments of the world took control of business in order to administer it for military purposes.

The moral and economic dislocation thus caused by the war must be regarded as a primary cause for the extravagant speculation, the abuse of industrial power, the neglect of industrial trusteeship that followed it. By the time the depression crept like a cloud over the world, the people had plenty of abuses to charge against industry and plenty of arguments for government regulation. In a desperate haste to achieve reforms they turned more and more to the government to run their affairs. In Germany, Italy and Russia the power given to the government is today complete. In England, France,* Canada and the United States the people still retain the ultimate power, but have encouraged the government to assume more and more responsibility for their jobs, their health, their old age, their security.

The cause of liberalism today, therefore, has changed. In the pre-war years we fought against domination of the people by Big Business. We now face the domination of the people by Big Government. I am not speaking of the United States alone, but of the trend which is apparent throughout the world. The liberal who fought against one kind of domination thirty-five years ago should find himself fighting against this new kind of domination today.

The liberal will, of course, be sympathetic with the principles of much of the social legislation of recent years, but the liberal will also be on his guard lest this trend go too far and suppress the individualism and

* Written May, 1938.

initiative which are the basic factors in the continuing advance of any civilization.

Remember that almost every time you have a necessarily complex law regulating an industry nowadays, you must set up a commission to administer it. We started with the Interstate Commerce Commission in 1887 and gave it new powers under Theodore Roosevelt in 1906. Then we had the Federal Trade Commission and the Federal Power Commission under Woodrow Wilson, and expanded the Federal Power Commission under Hoover. Since then, we have rapidly added others. . . .

So numerous are the departments, bureaus and commissions of all kinds now dominating the life of America that a year or so ago the United States Government began issuing an annual special directory for the guidance of the public. It names and describes eighty-two such departments and agencies, affecting almost every factor in the nation's life. We have more than one million Federal office-holders—not including any State office-holders—and at the last count they were increasing at the rate of 100 an hour a month or so ago. The salary list of the Federal Government now amounts to billions of dollars a year.

In number of employees, in salary payments, in annual budget, in scope of activities, here is the greatest corporation in the world. This corporation has what you might call a regular operating budget of about $3,-332,000,000, but it has a special budget of perhaps four billion dollars a year for public works, for unemployment relief, for agriculture.

The existence of Big Government on such a scale represents as much of a test of the true liberalism as did Big Business twenty-five years ago. The true liberal is as much opposed to excessive concentration of power in the hands of government as to excessive concentration of power in the hands of business. In other words, he maintains his freedom against all comers.

For example, in the period before the War, certain industries in the East grew fat on high tariffs. The liberal was opposed to these high tariffs because they were little more than subsidies given to a favored few. Likewise, today the liberal is opposed to subsidies given by the government to its own agencies for the purpose of competing with the people's business.

In the period before the War it was intolerable to the liberal that the corporation counsel of a railroad or manufacturer should have secret access to the Judge's chamber. Today, the liberal must condemn with equal vigor the statement by the present Solicitor General of the United States that, as Assistant Attorney General, he did his best to take his government cases to "a friendly court."

The true liberal would not tolerate such a thing as corporate efforts to influence the courts before the War. He will not tolerate executive or legislative domination in the courts today.

To the true liberal the attempt on the part of corporations to control legislatures was abhorrent. It must be equally abhorrent to him that a government should use for political purposes the enormous sums appropriated for relief.

The true liberal before the War was opposed to the efforts on the part of corporations to prevent their employees from organizing. And the true liberal today must be equally outraged when the government permits the Mayor of Jersey City to throw union organizers in jail—or eject socialists from the town—merely because the Mayor of Jersey City is Vice Chairman of the National Democratic Committee.

The true liberals today face exactly the same type of enemy under a different name that the liberals faced in the first fifteen years of this century. The difference is that the fight on behalf of liberalism in our times has become all the more important because liberalism has lost in perhaps half of the territory of the world.

When I was an undergraduate in Indiana, there were many nations under an autocratic form of government —many nations in which the rights of the people were respected either not at all or very little. But the trend at that time was toward freedom. Each year the people marched a little further ahead toward that goal. Then the War came, and for a short time freedom seemed to have won a victory. Old monarchies were destroyed. Territories were rearranged. Some half-dozen countries were put on the map which were not on the map in the University of my day. We even were arguing pro and con the advantages of a new principle in democracy—a democracy of nations, which would offer a method whereby the nations could settle their disputes in peace rather than by resort to war.

As I say, the trend was toward freedom; but today the trend has been reversed. At that time the institutions of monarchy and absolute control were under question. Today the institutions of democracy and individual liberty are under question. Mussolini, Hitler and Stalin believe the democratic form of government to be obsolete; they are convinced that their governments are far superior. They deprecate the cause of peace, maintaining that war offers certain advantages. They are opposed to free speech and a free press, claiming that censorship is for the good of the people.

If you are anxious to preserve the American system, therefore, you must be aware of the fact that there are those from outside who expect it to be destroyed and who will be glad to lend a hand in its destroying. "The struggle between the two worlds can have no compromise," states Mussolini. "Either We or They. Either their ideas or ours. Either our state or theirs."

If it is a question of either "We or They" certainly what "They" have does not compare, in all fairness, with what "We" still retain. We manage to pay our workers more, charge the consumer less, and make a better product than the manufacturers of any European country. Despite all the difficulties of recent years, we still have by far the highest standard of living; not only the highest in material comforts, but the highest in spiritual possessions; not only better machines, but more freedom. And we have achieved this because we have maintained the system of free enterprise under a democratic government. The surrender of liberalism to the theory of the totalitarian state would mean the sacrifice of the free man's achievement for a regulated and second-rate society.

So, just as I left the University of Indiana twenty-five years ago, sworn to defend the liberal cause, I return to it today pledged to the same purpose. The liberal cause is still in need of defense. I do not doubt that you will defend it. You could hardly spend four years here in this University, in this State, without absorbing a faith in the rights of man. Perhaps I should warn you, however, that liberalism is neither easy nor sensational. Very rarely is it called upon to storm the barricades with flags waving, and very rarely can it rely simply upon a good heart to determine the merits of its cause. Frequently you will find yourself in the minority, and sometimes you will find yourself alone.

The fact is that the liberal attempts to do the most difficult thing in the world—namely, to strike a true balance between the rights of the individual and the needs of society. He is like a man rowing a boat who when the boat swings to the right, pulls on the left, and when it swings to the left, pulls on the right. Liberalism sticks to the middle of the road, speaks quietly and insists upon the color of no man's shirt. If its voice seems small in the present tumult of shouting—if its ranks seem thinned among the regiments in uniform —let that be a sign to you, who have been educated in its spirit, to recognize the urgency of its cause.

FREE MEN

FREE MEN

An Address at the 44th Congress of American Industry, December 8th, 1939.

FREE MEN

By Wendell Willkie

THE history of government is the history of two conflicting principles: one is the supreme importance of the State; the other is the supreme importance of the individual. Either the people have believed that the State was merely the voluntary creation of individual citizens, responsible to them and designed primarily to protect their liberties; or else they have believed that the State was an authority in its own right to which individual citizens were subject and which could demand of them the suppression of their own desires and talents. *The individual versus the State*—that is the theme which more than any other has determined the course of civilization.

The distinction between these two philosophies is primarily one of *objective*. To those who believe in the State, the purpose of government is to increase its coercive powers, so as to regulate the way the people live. This distinction transcends in meaning all other political distinctions. We call England a monarchy, for example, and yet, ever since Magna Carta in the 13th Century, the rights of the individual in that country have been of greater importance than the authority of the State. On the other hand, we call ancient

Greece a republic, and history regards few governments as more efficient. But in ancient Greece, as in ancient Rome, the citizen belonged neither to himself nor to his family; he belonged to the State and was subject at all times to its peremptory and irrevocable demands. And in the very antithesis of monarchy—namely, communism—the State, as we have seen in Russia, owns the lives of the citizens completely.

It is not the form or title of government which determines its character; it is its purpose.

The conflict between these two philosophies—the individual versus the State—provided the impulse behind the formation of the United States of America. This country was founded on the idea that the individual is the source of the State's power and that the State was created *by* and *of* the men in it, and existed only to serve them. In fact, the United States is the only country which was organized on this principle from the very start. And, for the first century and a half of our existence, we were fortunate in living in a period when throughout the western world the doctrine of individual rights was gaining over the doctrine of absolute State power.

This is no longer true today. In modern Germany and Italy the leaders of the people proclaim the supremacy of the State. For a man to sacrifice his personal beliefs, his moral standards, his livelihood and his God for the sake of the State is regarded as a noble thing. For a woman to produce more and more babies for the armies of the State is an action to be rewarded

by a medal. Even the two greatest liberty-loving countries of Europe—England and France*—have now,
because of a war to fend their ideals, surrendered their
individual liberties and returned to an absolute government.

Today, the United States stands alone among the
great countries in its emphasis upon the rights of the
individual.

To my mind this spiritual isolation is no particular
cause for alarm.   I do not believe that we shall change
our faith by any action from without.   If we change it,
it will be because of some weakness within.   And even
then, we shall not change it directly.   It is bred in us
too deeply.   If we accept the doctrine of the authoritarian state, we shall do so gradually, indirectly, and
perhaps, even unconsciously. We shall do so with the
worthiest of motives. We shall say, for example:
"The newspapers print too much gossip, let the government censor them; our economic future is too uncertain,
let the government do the planning; it is too hard to
clean out our business stables, let the government do it
for us."   We shall bargain with the Devil for a short
cut to security.   We shall yield more and more of our
liberty under the delusion that we are giving it up only
temporarily until things get straightened out, and after
the deal is made, it will be too late. The Devil will
have gone off with our birthright.

"They that give up essential liberty to obtain a little

* Written December, 1939.

temporary safety," stated Benjamin Franklin, "deserve neither liberty nor safety."

There are many liberties which we in America regard as fundamental. But tonight we are talking specifically of the right of free economic enterprise. We have given the Federal government extensive powers over the economic and financial mechanism of this country in the past few years, and under these powers regulation was instituted in the name of *reform*. I believe that much of it was desirable, but now we need to be careful lest that power be used gradually, indirectly, to take away our liberties. We need to re-examine the relationship between the people's government and the people's industry on the basis of this question: Have we gone so far in regulating free economic enterprise that we have taken the life out of it?

Regulation has crept up on us steadily. The amount of it now imposed upon industry can be illustrated by the number of returns which must be filed with the Federal government. Last year the President appointed the Central Statistical Board to study this question. The report, of course, did not include the returns which an industry must file with any one of the 48 states in which it might happen to be located. To fulfill the Federal government's requirements alone, the Central Statistical Board reported that about 21,000,-000 returns of all kinds were filed for farms, making an average of approximately three returns per farm during the year. A total of 60,000,000 returns were filed by industrial, commercial and financial enterprises, not including farms, or an average of about 20 per enterprise per year. Each of these contained answers to an average of about 65 questions. Every return filed adds to the power of the Federal government over our private enterprise.

The most alarming feature of this concentration of power in the Federal government is the creation of omnipotent commissions to exercise it. The new fields of Federal control are administered by small Boards or executive commissions, usually appointed by the President and responsible to no one but the President. They are part of the Executive Department. But their function is not executive only. They have two additional functions: one is legislative, the other is judicial. These commissions write the rules which make the laws effective. Then they administer the rules; and when the rules are violated, they sit in judgment on the violators.

The Securities and Exchange Commission, for example, makes the rules for virtually all security financing throughout the country; for all of the country's stock exchanges; and for the financial operations of the utilities. When the rules are broken, the members of the Commission prosecute the offender and sit as judges to decide the penalties. In the same way, the National Labor Relations Board makes the rules governing collective bargaining and working conditions under the Wagner Act and then becomes both prosecutor and judge with respect to violations of that Act.

James Madison, who was chiefly responsible for the

Constitution of the United States, stated: "The accumulation of all powers—legislative, executive and judiciary—in the same hand . . . may justly be pronounced the definition of tyranny." And Lord Bryce said: "The separation of these powers is the fundamental characteristic of the American National Government and upon it depends the freedom of the individual."

Moreover, the rules prescribed by a commission involve the factor of uncertainty. Unlike the laws of Congress, they are not written in black and white upon the statute books. They may be changed at any time, at the commission's will. In the past five years there have been four chairmen of the Securities and Exchange Commission; and at each change the utilities and the stock exchanges and the corporations seeking capital have held their breath, waiting to find out what the attitude and policy of the new chairman would be.

For under commission regulation we do not have a government of laws. We have a government of men, and the conduct of an enterprise may be determined by the caprice of a commission chairman.

There isn't a man in this room who does not recognize the importance of the good will of Washington's commissions. There isn't a man in this room who does not know that if he criticizes a commission today, he and his company may suffer for it tomorrow. This is not a mere generality—it is a well-considered statement with abundant proof in my mind and your experience.

There are many who will say that State control in

America is different from State control in Europe because in Europe it is exercised by a despotic government in which the people have no voice. Seventy-five years ago this argument was answered by one of the greatest of the English liberals. "The real issue," Herbert Spencer said, "is whether the lives of citizens are more interfered with than they were; not the nature of the agency which interferes with them. . . . If men use their liberty in such a way as to surrender their liberty, are they thereafter any less slaves?"

Seven years ago the people of the United States set out upon what they thought was a great liberal campaign. They wanted to shake from their shoulders the burden of economic insecurity, of malpractices in business and finance, of wasteful speculation. They wished to control, insofar as possible, the conditions which limited the freedom of men.

Somewhere along the road we lost that objective. Instead of seeking to make men free—free to fight their own battle against poverty and fear and adversity under conditions that provided a fair chance to win— we decided to let the government fight the battle. The government wore the colors of the people's champion, but its conception of its function became authoritarian. It acted from the *top* on behalf of the people.

I believe that attitude to be a serious error. You will remember that democracy does not mean government *for* the people, only. As Lincoln was careful to point out, it means government *of* the people and *by* the people. The present government seems to have tried to take over the functions of America's free economic enterprises, instead of taking care that those enterprises should function honestly and encouraging them to function more efficiently.

Now and then in its relations with private enterprise the government has established a temporary "policy of appeasement," or "a breathing spell,"—pleasant little intervals between hostilities. And when we have optimistically believed these to be periods of government coöperation—some government official has sounded the trumpet for a new attack upon the people's industries. Each time the tired business man has settled down to his business, with a somewhat happier smile on his face, he has been roused by a new threat of government antagonism—much as the Egyptians used to carry around a mummy with the last course of every banquet to indicate that death was never very far away.

But government is not the only transgressor. Business, too, needs to mend its ways. For many years various sections of American industry have asked for special legislation which offered a temporary benefit at the expense of normal economic processes. Business has asked for special subsidies and special tariffs, for special protection against price cutters or low cost producers, for government appropriations for this or that special purpose. Business cannot ask for government interference at one time, and then indignantly reject it at another. And it hasn't been a pretty picture to see business, in the hope of advantage, craven and afraid to take its case to the people.

Moreover, we have witnessed within the past few years a rapid increase in the number of state tariffs and state regulations interfering with interstate commerce. Such action is suicidal. The greatness of the United States has depended partly upon this factor—namely, that it is the largest free trade area in the world. Here, again, business must take an interest in maintaining that free flow of commerce, from the lack of which Europe has so greatly suffered.

In the past few years the government has contributed some brave words and some moving phrases to the language of the American people. It has talked a great deal about "security." It has talked about "truth in the market place." It has talked about "economic planning" and "the more abundant life." These passwords have not admitted us into the promised land nor even into a land of promise; the unemployed still have no jobs and the young men have no dreams. It is true that the State has become rich indeed; but the people remain poor. The State has more power than it ever had before. The State spends eight billion dollars a year. The State, with 70 per cent of all the world's gold, has the largest buried treasure in history and one which is likely to be as profitless and as legendary as that of Captain Kidd.

All this the State has, but does the individual have more freedom and more opportunity, or less? The dozens of commissions and agencies and bureaus in Washington may have a more abundant life, but not the people whom they serve.

From now on, our purpose should be not to augment the powers of the State, but to increase the opportunities offered to the individual.   We are a hard-headed, practical race, and we have chosen the enterprise system as our way of life, not for sentimental reasons, but because it has created more benefits for more people in less time than any other.

BIG GOVERNMENT

BIG GOVERNMENT

Delivered before the Toledo Civic Forum and Rotary Club, Toledo, Ohio, on March 4th, 1940.

BIG GOVERNMENT

By *Wendell Willkie*

IF I had the time, I should like to write a history of
mankind's long struggle for freedom. It would begin
back in the shadowy reaches of the cave when men first
banded in groups to achieve a certain measure of freedom from the perils of the jungle. It would tell of the
wars of subject races to escape from a foreign yoke; or
the revolt of a people to overthrow the despots whom
they had themselves created. It would discuss the
methods whereby, in time of peace, men have sought to
protect themselves against the exercise of arbitrary
power, whether in the hands of the government, the
Army, business, or the Church. It would be a brave
story of men who prized their freedom above wealth
or power or security. And it would never be finished,
for freedom is like the breath of life itself: it cannot
be had and held forever; it must be continually recap-
tured and renewed.

When I was a young man in college, this nation was
engaged in a great liberal crusade. Its leaders were
three great Americans—all three very different in personality and background—Theodore Roosevelt, Robert
La Follette and Woodrow Wilson. Its objective was
to free the American people from the excessive power

of Big Business. "Let us ask ourselves very frankly what it is that needs to be corrected," said Woodrow Wilson. "To sum it all up in one sentence: 'It is the control of politics and of our life by great combinations of wealth.'"

American business corporations did not really get started until after the Civil War. The corporate form had, of course, existed for centuries before that date, but it was used chiefly for colleges, municipalities and other non-profit purposes, and later for trade and banking. It was not until the latter part of the 19th century that the manufacturing corporation began to flourish. This country was growing fast. Its basic industries, led by the railroads, were rapidly being organized into gigantic industrial combines, which sought to suppress all new competitors. The Sherman Anti-Trust Act in 1890 was not able to stem this mounting tide of economic power. The corporate monopolies began to extend their influence to the State Legislatures and even to Federal authorities. By the first years of this century they threatened to overshadow the people's government itself.

Then the liberals rose in alarm and began their long and colorful campaign to restrain this corporate power. Many of you will remember it, and many of you, like myself, undoubtedly fought under that banner. The oil trust, the tobacco trust, the beef trust and other monopolies were dissolved. The railroads discontinued the issuance of political passes. What Wilson called the "money trust" was destroyed by the Federal

Reserve Act of 1913. So successful was the campaign, that, in his message to Congress in 1914, Woodrow Wilson felt able to state:

Our program of legislation with respect to business is now virtually complete. . . . The road at last lies clear and firm before business.

Perhaps the restraints thus imposed upon corporate power would have been effective—perhaps the road would indeed have been clear for both business and the people—if it had not been for the World War. But wars are not good for freedom. They destroy the essential balance of society. They begin by giving dictatorial power to the government, and in the chaos that ensues after the war, this power will be passed from one hand to another, from one group to another, until once again, out of its agony, the spirit of a free people asserts itself.

In the inflation and false prosperity following the World War, business men, drunk with power, and a public, drunk with money, broke down the safeguards protecting individual liberties. When Sir James Bryce, the great critic of our civilization, wrote his concluding chapter of *The American Commonwealth* in 1920, he pointed out that "the growth of vast fortunes has helped to create a political problem," and warned us against "the irresponsible nature of a power which three or four men, or perhaps one man, can exercise through a great corporation." Rightly he prophesied that this would be an outstanding problem in those next few years.

In the money-mad period of the twenties the heads of some of our corporations forgot their primary function—that of running a business enterprise in a way that would be sound for the worker, the consumer and the investor. Instead of attending to the duties of management they began playing with corporate structures as with a child's building-blocks, becoming promoters rather than business men. And some financiers in Wall Street and elsewhere, instead of serving as a link between the savings of the people and the enormous capital needs of industry, became jugglers of finance, concerned primarily neither with the investor nor the investment, but with making money and securing power for themselves. There is no point now in naming names because this power and these positions are gone, and the men who wielded it are without influence. But you and I know that that was true. You have sat in Board rooms, as I have done, and heard business men talk about putting pressure on this man or this newspaper, or this or that group, so that opposition would be eliminated.

In the normal course of events we should have corrected that condition. Although the leaders of Woodrow Wilson's "new freedom" were no longer active, there were other men ready to take up that cause. But the depression overturned this corporate tyranny almost overnight.

For a while I hoped that the New Deal would replace it with a truly liberal faith. Certainly, no liberal movement ever had a greater opportunity, or was ever given more whole-hearted support by the people. But the leaders seemed to be motivated not by love, but by hate; they preferred to punish rather than to reform; they wanted to destroy the evil-doers, even if the doers of good should also succumb. For a time this lack of discrimination puzzled many of us, but it is puzzling no longer. Its explanation is found in the fact that the purpose of this new government was not to eliminate monopolistic control, *but merely to change its owner- ship.* Today it is not Big Business that we have to fear. It is Big Government. The abuses that cor- rupted the 1920's have been transferred from Wall Street to Washington.

Recall to your mind, for a moment, the abuses charged against business in the twenties. The first was the concentration of excessive power in the hands of a few men; second, the use of this power and the money that went with it, to influence political decisions; third, the manipulation of financial markets to the detriment of the investor and the enrichment of the manipulator; fourth, the ruthless determination to destroy opposition and create a monopoly.

Every one of those abuses exists today. We can re- peat each one of those accusations. But the respon- sible party today is not the nation's business, but the nation's government.

For example, on the first point, never before has this country experienced so extraordinary a concentration of power in the hands of a few men as in the govern- ment today. All of the safeguards erected by the

American people against too autocratic a government have been invaded. The powers once reserved to the states have been largely transferred to the Federal government. And the Federal courts, which have the responsibility for protecting the rights of these states or the rights of individuals against Federal legislation, have been largely staffed by appointees of the new system.

For a time the Supreme Court stood in the way of this political usurpation of power—so much so that the President undertook his notorious and unsuccessful campaign to force a change in its membership. But deaths and retirements gave to the President, by chance, what the people had denied to him by choice. And in the past three years, during which the President has been able to appoint five Supreme Court Judges, the American people have had a series of decisions from the Court that have substantially changed our form of government. On almost every decision the Court has supported the Administration. On almost every decision it has wiped out state and local lines and has extended Federal authority to every farm, every hamlet, every business firm and manufacturing plant in the country.

The Judiciary, therefore, has offered little check upon the network of laws which the Federal government has imposed upon the enterprises of the people.

I am not primarily concerned here with this change in the Supreme Court, nor with the extent of the regulatory laws, many of which are sound in principle and

most of which will never be removed from our statute
books.   I am primarily concerned with the method by
which these laws are administered.   In the old days,
laws were passed defining in black and white exactly
what those who were subject to them were supposed to
do.   But today, laws regulating national activities or
national industries must cover so many different and
complicated conditions that Congress cannot do anything more than prescribe the basic principles; it must
turn over to a commission the duty of formulating the
rules.

It would be obviously impossible, for example, for
Congress to write a law governing labor conditions
which would be applicable, without further interpretation, to every business or occupation, large or small,
anywhere in the country.   Such a law can only be written in general terms; a commission must be set up to
make it effective and to adjust it to different situations.
So the commission, in effect, writes the law.   The commission also prosecutes those who violate it.   Then,
having acted as both legislator and prosecutor, the commission undergoes another lightning change and becomes a judge sitting in judgment on its own case.

In the main, these commissioners are not appointed
by Congress.   They are not elected by the people.
They are appointed by the Executive and responsible to
him alone.   Thus the people have no control over
these individuals who write, enforce and judge the rules
for the 10,000,000 business enterprises of America.
Every business man in this room knows what this

means.   Whenever any one of you faces a commission regulation, or investigation, your first instinctive action is to classify the commissioners on the basis of those who are favorable to business and those who are hostile.

This is what is known as personal government.   It is the oldest form of government known to mankind. Perhaps you will remember the old Biblical story of Esther who served under King Ahasuerus.   When Haman had obtained from the King the authority to destroy Esther's people, Esther knew that her only chance for saving her people depended on winning the King's favor.   So she dressed in her most beautiful clothes and prepared a fine dinner for the King with much wine, and then she said: "If it please the King, and if I have found favor in his sight, and the thing seem right before the King, and I be pleasing in his eyes, let it be written to reverse the letters devised by Haman."

Too many business men have had to adopt that attitude with Federal commissions in similar circumstances.

This is perhaps as complete a statement of personal government as one could find.   For thousands of years mankind has suffered under government of that kind. And, in principle, there isn't much difference between that type of situation and the situation where the fate of an individual or an enterprise may depend upon the good will and favor of half a dozen Federal commissioners—or perhaps only one of them, if he is important enough to be the chairman.

Sometimes such a government has been honestly administered, sometimes dishonestly. But it is not the kind of government to be tolerated by an upright and independent people.

We have grown so hardened to the concentration of power in the hands of the Executive Department that we read, day after day, without a quiver, newspaper paragraphs discussing whether or not the President has decided to encourage private enterprise or whether he will continue the government's vast spend-lend program to add to the deficit and further delay investment confidence. It is no longer news that the decision of one man should determine the direction in which this country will move. In former days, in your city of Toledo you elected the officials who decided how the city's funds should be handled. Now, however, those decisions are largely made by someone in Washington over whom you have no control.

This concentration of political power in the hands of a few men not controlled by the people is just as bad as the concentration of economic power in the twenties; and it leads just as readily to the second abuse of which business was accused a decade ago—namely, the use of this power to influence political decisions.

I confess very frankly that this is a particularly sore point with me because I have personally been a victim of it so often. As most of you know, for several years the Commonwealth & Southern System, of which I am the head, was engaged in a fight to protect its operating companies in the Tennessee Valley from destruc-

tion by the government. We lost that fight, just as
every business will lose a fight against the government,
because we could not compete against a competitor with
political control over unlimited funds. To destroy our
business enterprises in the Tennessee Valley, and to
persuade municipalities to set up distribution systems of
their own, the government had two methods: first, the
Tennessee Valley Authority offered its power at a less-
than-cost rate, with the loss subsidized out of the Federal Treasury; second, the PWA would approach the
municipal authorities and offer to give them free 45
per cent of the cost of a new distribution system and to
lend them the rest at a very low interest rate.

Now, there is no legal corruption involved in this,
and obviously a municipal authority would find it difficult to refuse so tempting a proposal. But it represents one of many ways whereby an all-powerful
government can use its funds to influence political decisions.

Today there are thirty-one government agencies
which can lend money, and there are dozens of government commissions regulating industry. Coöperation
between the two offers frightening possibilities. A
couple of weeks ago the chairman of the National Labor Relations Board testified that the Board had an
arrangement with the Reconstruction Finance Corporation whereby that corporation would withhold any
loans to companies which the Labor Relations Board
had on its blacklist!

Personally, I think that various government officials

have made considerable effort to prevent the use of relief funds to influence the voters in political campaigns. Yet, we know that relief funds have been used in that way, just as they always will be where there is too much irresponsible political power. The influence of the purse is a great and grave influence, and a government which distributes millions of dollars on spend-lend programs holds a terrifying weapon over the heads of those who displease it.

No corporate body has ever exercised, or will ever be able to exercise, one-tenth of the influence upon a legislature that political money can impose.

And this brings us to the third abuse once lodged against business and now lodged against government— namely, the manipulation of the financial markets.

Not even a totalitarian state has more financial powers than those exercised by the present Administration. Such "rigging" of the markets as the bankers were able to achieve in their heyday in this country was as nothing compared with the financial puppet show put on by the government, in which, by pulling this string and that, the government can lower or raise interest rates, security prices, purchasing power and the value of various commodities.

For example, in 1934, in order to raise prices, the government decided to lessen the value of the dollar and increase the price of gold; so, since that time the government has been buying all the gold offered to it and paying a price of $35 an ounce. No other country and no other individual will pay such a price. If the

United States should withdraw its offer, the price would immediately fall.   As it is, the United States is slowly accumulating all the gold in the world.   In these days gold is dug up in South Africa only to be promptly buried in Kentucky.

The government has also set an artificial price for silver.   In the five years, 1934-1939, we spent about $1,160,000,000 buying 2,100,000,000 ounces of silver at a price far above its market value.   We did not need this silver, but the idea at first pleased the silver miners in two or three states.   It was not wholly pleasing, however, because it made the United States the only silver market in the world, so that our exports of silver, once a leading item in our foreign trade, were reduced to a negligible amount.

The government also maintains a stabilization fund of two billion dollars.   The operations of this fund are kept secret by the Treasury.   All that is known is that the Treasury uses these funds from day to day to buy and sell foreign exchange in order to keep the ratio at the level which it deems to be satisfactory.

The government also influences interest rates and security markets through the activities of the Federal Reserve Board.   There was a time when this Board was independent of the government.   Today, however, it is dominated by the United States Treasury. By open market activities through the Federal Reserve banks, interest rates, credit conditions and security prices generally are subject to the influence of the government.

Manipulation is defined as the deliberate interference with the free play of supply and demand in the security markets. Some of the government's manipulation has been desirable; some of its powers have been wisely used. But they represent a political domination of our finances beyond the wildest dream of the money-changers and economic royalists whom the President used to talk about. And there is little difference in method between the pools organized by individuals to force a security price up or down and the controls practiced by various agencies of the government to accomplish the same thing.

But these are only isolated items in this political domination of finance. Today the government, of course, has practically complete control of the banking system. Through the Securities and Exchange Commission it has control of the security markets where securities are bought and sold, and also control over the issuance of new securities. If the Securities and Exchange Commission does not like a bond issue, it can prevent it. I know this from personal experience.

These specific powers over money, over credit, over securities, over prices, etc., are perhaps of less importance than the government's general spending policy. When the government first started on its enormous expenditures for relief and public works, there was no question about their necessity. As emergency measures—and that was how they were regarded—they were sound and desirable. Unfortunately, because government rarely relinquishes a power which it has once obtained, the emergency character of these measures was shortly disregarded: the government embarked upon vast, continuing, spend-lend programs designed, not to promote private enterprise, but to promote direct financial and economic activity by the government.

But even the "spend-lend" phrase was found somewhat unsatisfactory. It was too tentative and temporary. Shortly the government began to talk about *permanent government investment.*

Today the popular phrase is "compensatory budget policy." In its complete form this policy calls for the government to increase its expenditures (and its deficit) when business is declining and to decrease them when business begins to recover. Government never likes to curtail a spending program; and the past seven years have demonstrated that government spending on so huge a scale does not stimulate business, but frightens it, and also frightens the investor who supplies our enterprises with their necessary capital. The government answers this by saying that ordinary investment methods are inadequate; the government should take over this function also. Mr. Adolph Berle very frankly defined this attitude in his memorandum before the National Economic Committee, which stated:

Briefly, the private financial system as at present constituted does not work. . . .

If, therefore, wealth is to be created by creation of government debt, the scope of government enterprise must be largely increased. Briefly, the Government will have to enter into

the direct financing of activities now supposed to be private;
and a continuance of that direct financing must mean inevitably
that the Government ultimately will control and own those
activities.

Manipulation of the markets in the old days was
child's play compared with manipulation by the government. Also, manipulation by business men or financiers at least was subject to government check. But
there is no check upon the government, except the people themselves.

The fourth charge which the liberals hurled against
the corporation presidents and bankers in the twenties
was that they created monopolies designed to eliminate all opposition. As business men, we have long
been familiar with the fact that the present Administration is intolerant of any opposition, however mod-
erate, to its reform measures. Laws are passed in an
atmosphere hot with hatred and splattered with epithets. Those who counsel moderation, or who propose amendments, are classed with the die-hards and
the Tories. As a result, many of the recent major
laws have caused a suffering that would be totally unnecessary if the Administration had accepted reasonable modifications. Far too often a perfectly sound
regulatory principle which might actually have been
helpful to the nation's welfare has been so distorted by
the government's desire for power, or its determination to punish, as to be harmful to the interest of the
people.

It is a curious feature of human nature that as a

man's power increases, so does his sensitivity to opposition.   We are familiar with the phenomenon of the
dictator who rages at the slightest reflection upon his
motives or his methods.   Messrs. Stalin, Hitler and
Mussolini are notorious for their dislike for anyone of
a skeptical nature; even the minor voices of opposition
disturb them.   The same weakness can be detected in
many members of the present government.   Public re-
bukes from the highest sources have been given to newspaper reporters who have become critical of Administration policies.   A chairman of one of the most
important Federal commissions has long followed the
practice of writing to, or calling upon, those newspaper
correspondents or editors who have seen fit to criticize
the chairman's actions.   Pressure upon the press is a
favorite weapon by which the Administration seeks to
silence the opposition—and to the credit of the press, it
is generally a futile one.

Incredible as it may seem, members of the present
Administration have seriously tried to label any form
of opposition as a sin.   I sat as chairman of a meeting at which the Secretary of the Interior, Mr. Ickes,
made a statement which would have astonished me even
more if I had not heard similar statements from similar sources.   Maintaining that opposition to the President was wicked, Mr. Ickes said:

> Anything you do at this time to shake the confidence of the
> great mass of the American people in either the President or
> the National Government is a sin against free enterprise, in-
> dividual liberty, political democracy and your own self-interest.

No matter on what you may disagree with him, he is now a symbol of confidence whose loss of symbolic value would now make all agreements and disagreements utterly unimportant.

There have been religious fanatics in the past who have gone out to slay all those who disagreed with what they were pleased to call the one true faith. Today different religions exist peacefully, side by side, and each recognizes the existence of differing creeds within it. It is the politicians who have become fanatic. The basic principle of a democracy is the perpetual existence of an opposition. Beware the government, however virtuous, that demands one hundred per cent acquiescence! The difference between a good tyrant and a bad one is only a difference in time.

You will remember that business fiercely resented the efforts made by the liberals to restrain the excessive powers of business. Big Business did not want to be checked in its control over the lives of the people. Now that the pendulum has swung the other way, we find that government has the same attitude. It does not want to be checked either. Just as business fought against regulation, so government today resists every effort to curb its authority.

For example, no trend in government has been more alarming than the growth of Federal commissions with what amounts to legislative, executive and judicial powers over industry, all combined in a few individuals appointed by the President. Last year the Senate Judiciary Committee reported to the Senate the Walter-Logan Bill requiring that the rules prescribed by these commissions should be issued only after public hearings and could not be put into effect until ten days after their publication; and requiring further that an orderly court procedure should be established for handling appeals from commission decisions. The Executive Department has opposed this Bill, just as industry in the old days resisted proposals for industrial regulation.

Too much power in the hands of a few men; use of money to influence political decisions; manipulation of the markets; destruction of all opposition—these were the charges hurled against the economic monopolies of the first quarter of this century. They are the charges which we make today against the present form of government. The banners used by the true liberals today are the same banners used by the liberals in that other time. They bear the same inscription; they make the same appeal; but the citadel of corporate power against which they once were led has fallen. It is a new citadel of entrenched political power toward which they must be directed.

You may remember that one of the problems faced by the heroes in the old Greek legends was the fact that their enemies so often changed their shape. Hercules, for example, once had to wrestle with a foe who, finding he was being defeated in the form of a man, instantly took the form of a serpent. As Hercules again began to master him, he assumed the form of a bull. The shape of the enemy continually changed, but the enemy remained.

The enemies of liberalism continually change their shape, but their hostility remains. The liberal fights an endless battle, sometimes against one form of repression, sometimes against another. But he knows that monopoly in any form is intolerable. For many years he fought it in the form of business: and lo! today it has changed its shape—it now wears the guise of government.

The people of the United States will begin their real recovery from the depression when they demand that a curb should be placed upon a government grown too great. In the past ten years there was only one major activity in this country which has shown any real expansion: that is the United States Government. Government employment has increased nearly 100 per cent; government expenditures have increased nearly 200 per cent, now amounting to over nine billion dollars; government borrowing has increased over 150 per cent. The government has created dozens of commissions and spent millions on buildings to house them. It has enormously added to its powers over our lives, and it has largely delegated those powers to Federal commissioners who are not responsible to the people nor to the Congress, but are appointed by the Executive.

Here is a real political boom! Here is one activity in which the enterpriser has become both rich and powerful. But all this has been accomplished at the expense of the people who have paid for it, not only in taxes, but in the losses which their enterprises have suffered as a result of this government activity. The

purpose of government is not to increase its own powers, but the powers of the people. The purpose of
government is to make men free. In his book, *The
New Freedom,* Woodrow Wilson made this memor-
able statement:

> The only thing that can ever make a free country is to keep
> a free and hopeful heart under every jacket in it. Honest
> American industry has always thriven, when it has thriven at
> all, on freedom; it has never thriven on monopoly. It is a
> great deal better to shift for ourselves than to be taken care
> of by a great combination of capital. I, for my part, do not
> want to be taken care of. I would rather starve a free man
> than be fed a mere thing at the caprice of those who are
> organizing American industry as they please to organize it. I
> know, and every man in his heart knows, that the only way to
> enrich America is to make it possible for any man who has the
> brains to get into the game.

Woodrow Wilson was talking about economic monopoly, but his statement is just as true when it is applied to political monopoly. If the Government of the
United States will sincerely dedicate itself to the purpose of making men free to carry on their economic
enterprises, and of making it possible for "the man with
brains to get into the game," then this country, with its
great trade area, its natural resources and its business
genius, will resume an economic progress which will be
even greater in the future than it has been in the past.

EVENING STAR OF THE GREAT DAY OF THE WHIGS

EVENING STAR OF THE
GREAT DAY OF
THE WHIGS

*BOOK REVIEW OF DAVID CECIL'S
THE YOUNG MELBOURNE*

*Reprinted from HERALD TRIBUNE
BOOKS August 27, 1939. Mr. Willkie
has in the past year written two book reviews for BOOKS, the literary section of
the New York Herald Tribune. The editors have selected one of them for reprint-
ing as an example of his scholarship and
wide range of interest.*

EVENING STAR OF THE GREAT DAY OF THE WHIGS

By *Wendell Willkie*

IT IS refreshing to read a book like this whose author poses no world problems, debunks no great reputations, and attempts to prove no social theory—but is content to make the final years of the Whig régime vivid and alive in a style lucid and engaging, with a scholarship exact but unobtrusive.

David Cecil is here primarily concerned with three Whig families and their influence in forming the character of one of England's least effectual Prime Ministers, the brilliant and beloved counselor of the young Queen Victoria. He deals not with the period of the premiership, however, but closes his account when, at the age of forty-seven, the young Melbourne, "smiling, indolent and inscrutable, . . . lay a pawn in the hands of fortune."

William Lamb, Lord Melbourne, was the evening star of the great day of the Whigs. By the first of the nineteenth century the Whig families were giving ground before a new and different type of leadership rising from the ranks of the manufacturers born of

the industrial revolution. It was this latter class that
was to force the social, economic and electoral reforms
of the nineteenth and twentieth centuries. The Whig
aristocracy, into which William Lamb was born, was
concerned with the maintenance of its own prerogatives. It had been the supporter of the Protestant suc-
cession, but it jealously resisted any effort on the part
of the Crown to extend the royal prerogatives. Out
of this struggle modern English parliamentary-cabinet
government was forged. On this largely was built the
great reputation of the Whig families which gave them
power for more than a century.

   With their wealth based upon their vast land holdings, the Whigs were as conservative in their other
political notions as they were liberal in their personal
conduct. Rooted in the soil, they had an earthly ex-
uberance, alongside which our present enthusiasms
seem pale. Rowdy, reckless and robust, they could eat
their twelve-course dinners, dance until dawn and gamble, drink and make love until breakfast—and still put
in a hard day's work on their estates or in Parliament.
The quality for which we envy them is not their morals,
which were questionable, nor their principles, which
were largely expedient, but their amazing vitality.
They had a zest for life and few reservations as to
when, where or how they should express it. Self-control
was not esteemed. The stiff-upperlip Englishman of
the public school—first popularized by Kipling and now
almost standard equipment in English fiction—would
have had no place whatsoever in their circle. As David

Cecil makes abundantly clear, the period of the great
Whig families was one of lusty enjoyments, of full-
flavored pleasures, of dangers taken with a relish.

It is not to be thought that this self-assurance, this
assumption that the world was theirs to enjoy, this fa-
cility for command, was easily achieved. It presup-
posed, of course, adequate financial resources—people
who could "jog along on £40,000 a year." The money
was seldom earned. It was either inherited or acquired by marriage. But without it a man was nothing.
As Lord Melbourne himself cynically phrased it in his
thoughtful and often witty note-book:

Wealth is so much the greatest good that Fortune has to
bestow that in the Latin and English languages it has usurped
her name.

But although the Whigs had money, they were never
the idle rich. The Whig was thoroughly prepared for
his career. Lord Melbourne, for example, spent many
years of his life in purely scholastic pursuits. At nine
years of age he went to Eton. At seventeen he entered
Cambridge. At twenty-one he went to Glasgow to live
for two years with a distinguished professor of philosophy. The severity of the Scottish régime is indicated
by his schedule: Study began after breakfast at 9:30
and continued with intermissions for lunch and supper
until 2:00 the next morning. Lord Melbourne was
well read in the classics and could and did discourse
on Pindar, Thucydides and St. Augustine with equal
ease. He could quote long sections of Shakespeare.
He wrote translations from the Latin and French

classics and created poetry of his own. Very early in his career his mother had seen to it that he had met all the great of his day, many of whom were her lovers, from the Prince of Wales to the brilliant playwright Sheridan, thus supplementing his formal education by his social contacts.

Lest such a summary should give the impression that William Lamb was a cloistered student and little else, perhaps it should be said that, like other reasonably well-born men of his time, he was as gay a blade as one could wish, and realistic enough to say, "What I like about the Order of the Garter is that there is no damn merit about it."

The formative influences in his life were largely feminine. His mother, Elizabeth Milbanke, married to a dullard and parvenu, Sir Peniston Lamb, by her own gifts became the acknowledged social leader of her time and spent the full force of a restless and calculating ambition in the formation of the character and the advancement of the careers of her children. "She was very beautiful in the style approved by her contemporaries, 'a fine woman,' with a clear-cut mouth, challenging dark eyes and a figure moulded in the shapely contours which stirred the full-blooded desires of the gentlemen of Brooks Club." She understood the art of getting on with men completely. "Level-tempered and rational, she found scenes and caprices as tiresome as they did. After the unaccountable moods of stormier sirens, it was infinitely delightful to find one's self 'laughing away an hour' on the sofa of her sitting-

room in Melbourne House, with Lady Melbourne—
Lady Melbourne, who could be depended upon never
to be touchy, or exacting, or shocked, or low-spirited,
who did not expect men to be monogamous, and who
never asked an awkward question. She seemed to com-
bine the social merits of both sexes, to possess, at the
same time, male robustness and feminine tact, a woman's voluptuousness and a man's judgment." Her chief
weapon was her power over men. "Characteristically,
she contrived that those she selected for peculiar favors
should be both agreeable and useful." During the
course of her career, her name was coupled with the
fashionable Lord Coleraine, the powerful Duke of
Bedford, and the faithless Prince of Wales. But the
most important man in her life was Lord Egremont,
by common consent of the times the father of Lord
Melbourne. In an atmosphere created and dominated
by such a mother, William Lamb was reared. And
David Cecil finds in this heritage the roots of the conflict in his character.

Even so, if he had married more wisely, perhaps he
would have used his exceptional equipment more effectively. His wife, however, was the wilful, pretty, tem-
pestuous Caroline Ponsonby, who, as Lady Caroline
Lamb, became notorious for her affair with Lord
Byron, whom Mr. Cecil sees not as the Don Juan of
his own imagination, or the Childe Harold that London
society adored, but as a cad, and a tawdry one at that.
The strong emphasis which Cecil places upon the con-
scious play-acting and cheap drama exhibited by both

Byron and Lady Caroline gives perhaps a more plausible explanation of the extravagances of the affair than is given in Maurois's *Byron,* or Elizabeth Jenkins's *Lady Caroline Lamb.* Because of her necessarily great influence upon the life of her husband, David Cecil spends much time on Lady Caroline, but even so, can only touch upon the high spots of a fantastically colorful and sensational career. There was no insanity too great for her to commit in the midst of one of her periodical love affairs. And that she was in fact half mad seems indisputable. In his description of her when Lord Byron finally retired, Mr. Cecil offers one of the many brilliant pictures with which the book is starred:

Ghastly pale, bone thin, and with eyes starting from her head, she looked insane, and throughout the winter, derangement also betrayed itself in a series of actions, fantastic, ludicrous and distressing. She offered herself to young men on condition that they challenge Byron to a duel; she forged a letter from Byron to a picture-dealer in order to get possession of his portrait; she put her men servants into a new livery, on the buttons of which were engraved "Ne crede Byron"—Do not believe Byron. But her most singular performance was a bonfire at Brocket, on which Byron's presents to her were solemnly burnt, while some village girls dressed in white capered round the flames in a ritual dance of triumph, and a page recited verses composed by Caroline for the occasion.

Curiously enough, despite these passionate episodes with an array of reputable and disreputable people, despite her ostracism from society, William remained her last as well as her first love. It is a tribute to the loyalty of his nature that he could not bring himself to

abandon her, and to the power of her fascination for
him, that she could always charm him, however exas-
perated and humiliated he might be. And perhaps the
best summary of her full and fatal life is found in her
own words: "I seem to have lived a thousand years and
feel I am no wiser, better nor worse than when I
began."

William Lamb's tendency toward indecision, toward
a neutral tolerance that later often rendered him in-
effectual, was undoubtedly heightened by the turmoil
which had continually existed in his home. Although
he entered Parliament as early as 1805, his public career did not achieve any particular importance until
after his wife's death in 1828. It is at this point that
David Cecil leaves him—having clearly indicated the
conflicting elements in his character.

Melbourne did not, of course, believe in reform, although, ironically enough, when he finally did come into
power, it was as the head of a popular government.
Nevertheless, he uttered an admonition which American business might have profitably observed in 1933.
"Those who resist improvements as innovations," he
said, "will soon have to accept innovations that are not
improvements."

This book is not a biography. It is primarily a study
of the social and political influence at work upon Melbourne in his formative years, and more space is given
to the people who surround him than to the man himself. The author too modestly calls his study a "conversation piece." It is, more accurately, a fascinating

introduction to a man and his time—so fascinating that the reader is left unsatisfied with this volume and cries for more.   It would be especially interesting to see whether David Cecil's interpretation of Melbourne in later years would differ from Lytton Strachey's appealing picture of Lord Melbourne as the friend and confidant of the young Queen Victoria in the full tide of his power.

It may be true, as the young Melbourne, who loved to deal in paradoxes and "defend the indefensible" would say: "It is a good thing when these authors die, for then one gets their works and is done with them." Here's hoping, however, that one who writes as David Cecil does gives us many more works before we are "done with" him.

SOME OF THE ISSUES
OF 1940

SOME OF THE ISSUES OF 1940

An address delivered at the Waldorf-Astoria, April 25, 1940, before the Bureau of Advertising, American Newspaper Publishers Association.

SOME OF THE ISSUES
OF 1940

By *Wendell Willkie*

THIS dinner of the American Newspaper Publishers Association gives me an opportunity to correct a minor misconception. Within the past few days several newspapers have referred to me as a possible "dark horse" for the Presidential nomination. Naturally, I felt very much honored by this reference and was as interested in it as any other American citizen would be. A friend of mine, however, showed me the definition of "dark horse" as supplied by Sir James Bryce in his great book, "The American Commonwealth." Discussing American politics, Lord Bryce said: "Speaking generally, the note of the Dark Horse is respectability verging on colorlessness; and he is therefore a good sort of person to fall back upon when able but dangerous favorites have proved impossible."

Perhaps I should not really object to the word "respectability," although it alarms me a little. But it is not as disturbing as the term "colorless." I sincerely hope that that definition is not what my friends had in mind in using the phrase.

But, seriously, my interest in present-day discussions

—and I consider them to be of critical importance to this country—is not a personal one; it is to win popular support for certain principles in which I believe.

Now, these are days when every man calls himself a liberal. Republicans, Democrats, New Dealers, Socialists, Communists, business men, artists, young men or old men, rich men or poor men—they all claim the label of liberalism. In my business travels around this country in the past two or three years I have met and talked with hundreds of people of very different kinds, and not one of them was a conservative.

ONE COMMON QUALITY OF ALL WHO CALL THEMSELVES LIBERALS

It is, of course, impossible to define the term "liberal" so that it will include all of these groups. Somebody, somewhere, is out of line. But if we cannot arrive at an acceptable definition for liberalism, we can certainly agree upon one common quality—one fundamental characteristic—without which no man can have a shadow of a claim to the title. The liberal is a man who believes in freedom for himself and for other people.

If the results of freedom were not satisfactory in terms of human welfare, it would no longer be a wise policy for the world to follow. Economic freedom can mean very little to a man who is starving. If free economic enterprise is unable to provide jobs and products for this country, then, obviously, some other system should be tried. It seems to me that it is on this point that the liberal and the reactionary really find their issue.

The liberal believes that the purpose of government is to make men free and, thus having freedom, men will be able to build up a productive and prosperous society. The reactionary may desire, with equal sincerity, a prosperous society, but he believes it can be achieved only by the concentration of economic or political power.

This is the issue that the President threw into the ring last Sunday in talking to the Young Democrats. From his viewpoint, he made the issue very simple : all New Dealers are liberal; all others are reactionary. Since this issue of liberalism will be the fundamental issue underlying all the arguments in this Presidential campaign and since our conception of liberalism is embodied in a democratic government, let us consider for a moment the purpose of such a government.

The free democratic system which we enjoy in the United States and which is now being so severely tested by the critical situation at home and abroad, has had a relatively short life in the world's history—no more than a century and a half. The beginnings of the democratic principle, however, go far back to the beginnings of civilization. The democratic principle is based upon the dignity of man. It acknowledges certain inalienable human rights. It asserts a faith in individual liberty as against the supremacy of the state. No one knows when that principle first stirred the minds of men; but its outcry has been found carved in stone, or inscribed on papyrus, or painted on clay in the discovered remnants of civilizations that go back at least 7000 years.

Birth of Democracy

But it was a long time before these gestures toward a free society developed into actions, and a still longer time before these actions, in turn, became translated into achievement. The Renaissance was the first great revolution to quicken the Western World with the idea, largely inherited from Christianity, that every human being is, and of right ought to be, free.

This was a truly radical idea at the time. In many countries it would be considered radical today. It was vigorously combated by the ruling powers, and many who believed in it were thrown into prison, tortured, forced into renunciation. The birth pangs of democracy were severe. But the democratic faith grew stronger, flaring into small victories here and there in each century, until it celebrated its great triumph in America with the founding of a new type of government, deriving its powers from the people, with individual liberty protected under law.

The First Phase of Democracy

I would call this period leading up to the nineteenth century the first phase of democracy. Its purpose was to make men free. Democracy in this first phase was designed to protect a small handicraft society engaged in local enterprises from excessive political interference. It did this so well that the economic progress made by this society has never been equaled in any other country. It promoted a spirit of energy, daring and imagination which transformed this small people into a great nation in less time than most states have required merely for stabilization. It created a people teeming with ideas, full of invention, boundless in optimism and tireless in effort. In fact, this economic progress was the factor which made a change in government necessary.

DEMOCRACY'S SECOND PHASE

Even while the first phase of democracy was writing its principles in the Constitution of the United States, the second phase, destined to change the application of those principles, was beginning. The dominant influence in this second phase was the industrial revolution, which substituted the machine for hand labor. The man who had worked at home by himself now worked with others in a small factory. Collective action took the place of individual action. Men came from other towns to get jobs. Products were shipped to other towns to find a market. The organization of an enterprise took in more and more people over a wider and wider area.

This created a new problem for democracy. Statutes designed to cover half a dozen men working on a job in one community were inadequate for the problem cre-

ated by 50,000 men in an enterprise operating in half a
dozen states for a national market. Some of these
enterprises had budgets bigger than the budgets of the
states themselves. Their policies might affect the welfare of several state populations. They made or unmade towns. They made or unmade political careers.
The economic enterprises of the people, in this second
phase, waxed so great as to tower over government
itself.

Third and Final Phase

It is at this point that the third phase of our democracy begins. It is the final phase and the one which will
determine whether or not democracy, as a method of
government and a way of life, can endure. It is the
phase in which the democratic process must arrive at a
solution between the regulation of the people's enterprises, on the one hand, and the preservation of their
independence, on the other. It represents, in effect, an
adjustment between the Renaissance and the industrial
revolution.

The great liberal movement of the early twentieth
century, led by such men as Theodore Roosevelt, by the
elder Robert M. La Follette and Woodrow Wilson,
was the expression of an effort to make this adjustment.
The last of these great leaders, Woodrow Wilson, in
the program for what he called "the new freedom,"
thought that this adjustment had been made. Perhaps
the program would have succeeded if it had been organized at a normal period in the world's history. Un-

fortunately, the time was not normal: the next year the world was plunged into a war. When it was over, the liberal faith, which is always one of the first casualties of war, was slow to recover. The United States was rich. People were making money. Industry was expanding so fast that there wasn't time to think about controls. A few men in business and in banking managed to concentrate in their hands an enormous amount of money and influence, and the investor, the employee and the consumer began to feel helpless before their secret manipulations.

It is clear now that the system of 1929 could not be permitted to stand. Democracy in this third phase needed more social controls. These the New Deal supplied, in a vast network of regulation. The liberal cannot object to these reforms in principle. He realizes the national character of the great American corporations and of many business and financial operations; he realizes that an extension of Federal authority is necessary to establish adequate control over these matters. It is certainly a proper question for the defenders of the present government, therefore, to turn to him and say, "If you are opposed to this government, what powers would you take away?"

For example, the conscientious liberal would surely not rescind Securities and Exchange Commission acts and return that regulation to the states. He would not demand that the Federal government keep its hands off interstate utilities or utility holding companies. He would not challenge the wisdom of having the right of collective bargaining recognized by law. He would not say it was no concern of the Federal government whether or not the aged had pensions or the worker had unemployment allowances. In fact, the liberal would find himself in agreement with most of the objects of this new legislation, although he might want to modify many of its provisions and change many of its methods.

What attitude, then, does the liberal take toward the present government?

The answer is what it has always been. To the liberal the purpose of government is unchangeable. It is to leave men free. Whether democracy is in its first phase or its second phase or its third phase, that is the objective.

New Concept of Government

And the liberal does not see in the present Administration any will to leave men free. He sees only an attempt to increase the powers of government. For the old American principle that government is a liability to be borne by the citizens for the sake of peace, order and security, the New Deal has substituted the notion that government is an asset without which none of us can survive. The present huge Federal organization with its payroll of over a million employees, its dozens of agencies and commissions, its expenses of several billion dollars a year, represents an entirely new concept of government. It is government regarded, not as a supplementary influence, but as a dominant force in the lives of the people. Its growth becomes desirable in itself, instead of desirable only if it promotes the ease and expansion of the people's activities, the happiness and independence of their lives. Our forefathers believed that progress came from the energies of the people: the function of government was merely to prevent those energies from getting out of bounds. Today the government publicly proclaims the failure of the people's enterprises and has adopted the principle that progress comes from government itself.

This hostility toward domestic business is the more extraordinary in view of the government's friendly attitude toward foreign trade. Without entering here into technical arguments as to methods by which they are to be brought about, international trade agreements which lead to further interchange of goods between nations and the establishment of an international monetary standard are, in my opinion, indispensable to our complete recovery and future economy. America might live without international trade, but only with an economy managed either by business monopolies or government control. Likewise, despite recent pronouncements to the contrary by some opposed to the present Administration, we do have a vital interest in continuance of the English and French way of life.

TAXES AND BUSINESS

If we examine this government's domestic activities —government regulation, the tax program, the spending program—we find no evidence of any desire to promote the businesses of the people. Neither the New Dealers, who wrote the laws regulating business enterprises, nor the commissioners who now administer those laws seem to be interested in encouraging business. We have heard a lot about abuses. We have seen one industry after another summoned before hearings, and this or that corporation charged with violations of a commission rule. But we have not heard anything about the welfare of the people's enterprises. The government does not seem to care whether its laws have made business more dead than alive. Clearly, a law regulating an industry should aim to make that industry function more efficiently for the public welfare. But in the past eight years, have you ever heard a government official ask the question: Is this industry more healthily active since we started regulating it?

And the same spirit lies behind the government's tax program. Taxes in this country are high. But it is not the amount of the tax that hurts business as much as it is the kind of tax. Taxes must always be somewhat restrictive to business expansion and investment. They act as a brake upon the flow of money into new undertakings. But the basis of a scientific tax program is to raise the necessary money for government with the least possible interference with the enterprises of the people. Admittedly, that is not the purpose of the present tax program. The idea has been to "soak the rich" or "to redistribute income" in order to force certain reforms. As a result, our tax system tends to dry up the sources from which industry gets its capital. For example, we have the highest tax on large incomes of any country in the world. Ours is the only government in the world to impose a tax on capital gains as income. And, having imposed a tax on capital gains, the government grants only partial allowance for capital losses. The result is that those who have money to invest in enterprise prefer to buy government securities which are exempt from taxation. In effect, therefore, the tax system rewards the man who plays safe and penalizes the man who takes a chance. And it is the man who is able and willing to take a chance who provides new industries and new jobs.

Your own industry, like all industries, started that way. Exactly 500 years ago a skilled metal worker named Johann Gutenberg had an idea for printing from movable type. He is reported to have been a wealthy man. He had exhausted his own resources in the development of this idea, and he needed more money. Here was a highly risky enterprise. The printing press was just a wild man's dream which, incidentally, would put out of work those scribes who wrote out their manuscripts in long hand or those who worked from wood blocks. Such a man could offer no gilt-edge security for people who had to play safe. His venture could only appeal to some one willing to take a chance. Fortunately an investor was found—one Johan Fust—who advanced to Gutenberg large sums of money for his experiments. Like two-thirds of the new development in this country, this one failed. The loans were never repaid, and the investor eventually took over Gutenberg's equipment and with it produced the Gutenberg Bible that will be forever associated in men's minds with the great invention of printing.

New ventures may have enormous possibilities; but they are always attended by great risks. Only the man of means can take those risks, and he must be compensated by the incentive of profit. The tax program should not be designed to punish the man with money, but to make his money useful.

"SPEND-LEND PROGRAM"

The government can hamper industry, not only by the way it collects its money, but also by the way it spends it. The government, of course, has always had a spending program. In earlier days it gave land away to settlers and provided the railroads with rights of way. It gives subsidies to shipbuilders and airplane manufacturers. It has spent billions of dollars on roads. But in each instance these expenditures were made for specific purposes and to stimulate private enterprise. They were not undertaken simply for the sake of government spending or simply for the sake of keeping government in a business.

When the depression occurred, there were certain essential expenditures which the government had to make for relief. No government could possibly have avoided spending money to keep people from starving. And there were certain very large expenditures made for recovery purposes. These were recognized as of an emergency nature. They were proposed as such and approved as such. But the emergency label has been dropped. These expenditures are now part of what is apparently a permanent "spend-lend program." Sometimes this spending is directly competitive with business. Sometimes it is indirectly competitive: it frightens capital and destroys business confidence by increasing the government debt and deficit and requiring continued high taxes. Whether directly or indirectly competitive, this spending is opposed to the expansion of industry. No one expects the budget to be balanced right away, or the debt to be wiped off by some fiscal magic. But the people ask for some indication that the government will at least aim for that objective.

Our attitude toward these things was best defined perhaps by the President himself in the speech in which he supported the now forgotten 1932 platform, with its pledges to abolish "useless commissions and offices, consolidating departments and bureaus and eliminating extravagance" and "to recover economic liberty." He said:

"Any government, like any family, can for a year spend a little more than it earns. But you and I know that a continuation of that habit means the poorhouse."

The theory that the government must take control of the economic functions of the country has never received clearer statement than that given to it by a spokesman for the present Administration, who presumably ranks second only to the President himself.

Two weeks ago at America's Town Meeting of the Air, the Attorney General of the United States was debating the topic "What Are the Essential Differences Between the Republican and the Democratic Parties?" Mr. Jackson struck another blow at the idea that any of the government's present powers were of an emergency nature, or were considered to be temporary. He stated: "We must complete a long-term program to take the place of short-term remedies and emergency experiments." He maintained that the government's responsibility was to provide "economic opportunity and security," and he remarked with some surprise:

"The real powers in the Republican party contend, and I think that they honestly believe, that economic opportunity and security for the great majority of our citizens are unattainable by government effort."

Basis of Free Enterprise

I cannot speak for "the real powers of the Republican party." But I hope that Mr. Jackson has defined their attitude correctly, for personally I do, indeed, contend and believe that "economic opportunity and security for the great majority of our citizens are unattainable by government effort." In fact, the free enterprise system is based on just the opposite thesis. We have believed that economic opportunity and security for the great majority of our citizens will never be attainable through the government and are only attainable through free private enterprise. In the past 150 years we have gone a long way toward proving it.

Government has never created an invention, never founded an industry and never successfully operated a business. Our quarrel with the New Deal is on exactly the issue defined by Mr. Jackson: whether the government or the people shall manage the people's enterprises.

Well, we have given the government eight years to prove its theory and it has failed to do so. One-third of the nation is still in need. Ten million men are still unemployed. The deficit continues to increase. The people, I hope, are now ready to try again the other theory: to release the enterprises of the people from the terrific weight of bureaucracy and to rededicate the government to the purpose of leaving men free. This does not mean, as Mr. Roosevelt suggested in his speech to the Young Democrats, a return to the 1929 way of life. The country's liberals are not all in Washington.

In a time of bitter argument, it is often helpful to turn to an outside expert who has no connection with either side of the controversy and whose opinion is, therefore, unemotional and unbiased. The internationally known magazine "The Economist," of London, belongs in that category. In a recent issue "The Economist" discusses the theory that the United States "is growing old" and says that "It is difficult to take this theory seriously—or to know whether its partisans themselves take it seriously." "The Economist" raises this question:

"If the United States with its vast areas, its low debt, its inexhaustible natural resources, its rising population is a mature economy, what is Great Britain? And yet our 'decadent' economy has contrived, during the decade when America was standing still, to go ahead as fast as on the average of the great Victorian era of expansion. Ten years ago the per capita national income of the United States was one-third larger than the British. Today it is probably no larger at all. . . . The American economy seems to have forgotten, for the moment, how to grow. But the probable explanation of this economic anemia is to be found not in any arrival at 'maturity' but rather in the existence of institutional obstructions to a free flow of capital."

For the development of any economic enterprise three human factors are fundamental. The first is the inventor, who has the idea for a new device or a new method or a new product; the second is the investor, who has sufficient confidence in the inventor's dream to give him the necessary capital to develop it; the third is the administrator or manager, who can organize the business and keep it going.

I believe that we have more men in these three categories in America today than ever before in our history. We have always been an inventive nation. We spend several hundred million dollars a year on industrial research. Last year we patented 43,000 inventions. And there are plenty of potential investors. Never before in the history of the country has there been so much money lying idle in the banks. In these two categories of invention and investment, the condition of abundance can be statistically proved. I have no statistical proof for the condition of the third factor of business management, but I have this personal conviction: that never before in American history have there been so many business executives who are not only skilled in the technique of running their jobs, but who have a new and far more enlightened attitude toward their social responsibilities.

These three types of men have constituted the triumphant triumvirate of our economic past. They are equally important to our future. Their activities, if released from government restrictions, can provide jobs enough and products enough to restore prosperity to America. But first we shall have to remove the political restrictions. The activities of the present Administration have drained the vitality and confidence from American industry. It is ironic that in view of these conditions the government should then turn upon industry and denounce it for its failure to recover and make wild charges concerning a "strike" of capital. Industry is being criticized for being unable to do what government prevents it from doing.

TASKMASTERS OF EGYPT

This is a technique long in use. It is described in the oldest recorded campaign for freedom in history—that of the people of Israel against the tyranny of Egypt. You may remember the story. Several thousand years ago when the people of Israel were in bondage in Egypt, Pharaoh called his taskmasters together and said: "Let us give the people no more straw for their bricks. But at the same time tell them they must make as many bricks as before." So the taskmasters took away the straw. The people were unable to make bricks. The taskmasters summoned their leaders and beat them. The leaders protested to Pharaoh, crying out: "Wherefore dealest thou thus with thy servants? There is no straw given unto thy servants, and they say to us, Make brick: and, behold, thy servants are beaten; but the fault is in thine own people."

But Pharaoh said, "Ye are idle, ye are idle: Go therefore now and work; for there shall no straw be given you, yet shall ye deliver the tale of bricks."

The story is not different today. The taskmasters in Washington have taken away that freedom of economic enterprise which is as vital to recovery as straw was to the making of bricks. And then they have turned on the leaders of these enterprises and blamed them for unemployment and depression. But in the words of the people of old we say: the fault is in thine own people.

WITH MALICE TOWARD NONE

WITH MALICE TOWARD NONE

Reprinted from

THE *SATURDAY EVENING POST*,

December 30th, 1939.

WITH MALICE TOWARD NONE

By *Wendell Willkie*

LIKE other businessmen, I have had to spend many days in Washington in recent years. And at the end of those smoke-filled, strained and wordy afternoons, I formed the habit of driving from the Washington Monument past the Lincoln Memorial to the home of Robert E. Lee, at Arlington. It was a trip that was unfailingly refreshing, not only because of its physical beauty—the tall shaft of the monument piercing the sky; the classic temple and lagoon with its great, brooding, gentle figure; the fine proportions of Lee's home—but also because of a certain spiritual significance I found in it; for the greatness of these three men—and they were perhaps the three greatest which this country has produced—had a common quality: Each had a genuine love of his fellow men, and a magnanimity even for those who opposed him.

"With malice toward none," Lincoln said; "with charity for all."

"I have fought against the people of the North because I believed they were seeking to wrest from the South dearest rights," said Robert E. Lee. "But I have never cherished toward them bitter or vindictive feelings, and have never seen the day when I did not pray for them."

"Without more charity for the opinions and acts of one another in governmental matters," Washington said, "I believe it will be difficult, if not impracticable, to manage the reins of government, or to keep the parts of it together."

It is, to my mind, a tragic reflection on our times that I have heard no one of our political leaders express any sentiment like these in recent years. And the importance of it lies in this fact: That without this magnanimity, this tolerance for mankind, there can be no such thing as a liberal faith. The leaders of government today have flaunted their theory of liberalism more widely than any other government in our history, but they have said nothing about tolerance; they have, in fact, drained the vials of invective against all who have opposed them. They have founded their liberalism on hate, and a liberalism which has its roots in hatred bears the fruit of tyranny.

Let us consider for a moment the nature of liberalism. It has been defined by various men as an attitude of mind. Others have objected to this definition as being too passive; they have pointed out that liberalism may also be a program of action. Certainly, action is an essential part of any faith, but I shy from that word "program" because there seems to be no such thing as a fixed and predetermined program for a liberal. What may be a liberal procedure at one time and in one place may be the opposite in another.

A liberal in New York City, for example, is almost certain to regard things quite differently from the liberal, let us say, in Kansas. In New York City he believes strongly in "personal liberty." By that he is apt to mean, among other things, the right to buy and sell intoxicating liquor or cigarettes, for example. In Kansas, however, he may believe primarily in "personal purity." Hence he may be opposed to the liquor business or the cigarette business, on the assumption that it menaces the condition of purity and makes it more difficult for men to be "free" of evil; and in Nebraska the great liberal, George Norris, supported prohibition. Likewise, liberalism in any great metropolitan area may mean lower prices for food, but in the country it may mean higher prices for food crops. Liberalism may guide men of equal wisdom to very different courses of action. Washington and Lincoln fought for the creation and preservation of the American Union; Lee fought for the preservation of the individual state. And yet all three of them were men of liberal faith.

And so, feeling that a universal program for liberals is impossible, I have asked myself what is the common denominator for those of liberal faith. The answer seems to me to lie in the common purpose of liberals to make men free. For it is not the primary purpose of the liberal to make men secure or rich or powerful, but only to prevent such limitations upon freedom as insecurity, poverty and weakness may impose. There are

worthy causes other than this one of human freedom—
"security," for example, is now a very popular one
—but, in my opinion, they are not so important—they
are not fundamental. In other words, the liberal is one
who prefers, as Newton Baker once stated it, "to be
poor, if necessary, but in any case free."

Just as the true liberals of the world have a common
purpose, so they have a common quality. That quality
is love of humankind. The true liberal does not fight
for a cause because of a desire to punish those who
have a different way of looking at things and doing
things. Instead, the true liberal fights for a cause
which he feels will be of as much value to his opponents
as to himself. The dictator who has his opposition
shot in order to put through any number of liberal
laws, for example, can hardly claim the title of liberal.

"Liberalism," said Ortega y Gasset in *The Revolt of
the Masses,* "is the supreme form of generosity; it is
the right which the majority concedes to minorities, and
hence it is the noblest cry that has ever resounded in
this planet. It announces the determination to share
existence with the enemy."

In 1932 I believe that this nation was ready for the
greatest liberal campaign in its history—an emancipa-
tion greater than that of the slaves, because it had to
do with all men, regardless of color. The people were
waiting for a leader who would lead them out of the
panic, confusion and despair of the times; they were
seeking a way whereby they could lift from their backs
the burden of economic insecurity, of malpractices in

business and finance, of discontent in the ranks of labor. They wished to control, so far as possible, those conditions which limited the freedom of men. And to their leader they gave, in an outburst of enthusiasm and confidence, more power than has ever been given to a Government of the United States. But today they have not achieved that freedom. They are like an army which started out triumphantly for a certain objective, which now, bewildered, finds itself following its leader in an entirely different direction.

For what has become of the great causes which we were to serve? We were to improve working conditions and make industrial relations more amicable; and by partisan procedure we have fomented industrial strife and increased the difficulties of re-employment. We were to provide social security, both for the employed and for the aged; and we wrote into the laws such drastic and unnecessary provisions as to place a tax upon employment and to make pension funds available for political purposes. We were to impose certain regulations upon industry which would prevent the abuses of the past, and we created a network of Government bureaus and rules which have taken the life out of industrial enterprise.

We were to make the security exchanges of the country free and efficient market places where the people could buy and sell their stocks and bonds; but we have so hampered the exchanges with restrictions as to impose innumerable difficulties in the way of both the buyer and the seller. We were to require "truth in securities," so that the public no longer would be misled by the misstatements of the unscrupulous few; instead, we have made the requirements for new security issues so exacting, so complicated and so voluminous that the information obtained is of no practical value to the buyer, and creates enormous expense and uncertainty for the seller.

All these causes were good. All of them were designated to serve the great objective of liberalism—namely, to make men free. What happened to them on the way, to distort their purposes and corrupt their results?

We must go back to the essential quality of liberalism. The leaders of the past few years have founded their liberalism in hate of men, not in love of mankind. The announcements of reforms have been shrill with the denunciation of all those groups and individuals who opposed them or the manner of them.

For their special attack, our liberal leaders have singled out those men who throughout this nation's industry have most dramatically represented the spirit of individual initiative and free enterprise—namely, businessmen. They sought to provoke one class against another and used the misconduct of a few as an excuse for vituperation against the many.

As you look back through the tremendous changes in recent years, can you recall any Government leader who has risen to say: "With malice toward none?" Or anyone who has confessed that he prayed for his enemy and never cherished toward him "bitter or vindictive

feelings"?   Or one who asked for "more charity for
the opinions and acts of one another in governmental
matters"?

Such words as these have a strange and beautiful
music as compared with the harsh discords of reform
in the past few years.

Now, I do not believe that this change in the temper
of men will last. We have been bitter, indeed, and we
are surrounded by continents of bitterness. But liberalism—in the realm of government we call it "democracy"—is still the faith of this country. And if the
recent procedures in its name are reconsidered in the
spirit of the three men who have most profoundly affected our lives, we shall once more be pursuing the
liberal purpose—to make men free.

WE, THE PEOPLE:
A PETITION

WE, THE PEOPLE: A PETITION

*Reprinted from FORTUNE, April, 1940.
This Petition was printed as the conclusion
of an article called "We, the People, A
Foundation for a Political Platform for
Recovery" in "Fortune," April, 1940. It
has since been reprinted and editorialized
all over the country.*

WE, THE PEOPLE:
A PETITION

Before the political platforms are written, We, the
People, have a declaration and a petition to make

IN THE decade beginning 1930 you have told us that
our day is finished, that we can grow no more, and that
the future cannot be the equal of the past. But we, the
people, do not believe this, and we say to you: give up
this vested interest that you have in depression, open
your eyes to the future, help us to build a New World.

IN THIS decade you have separated "business" and "industry" from the ordinary lives of the people and have
applied against them a philosophy of hate and mistrust,
but we, the people, say: business and industry are part
of our daily lives; in hurting them you hurt us. Therefore abandon this attitude of hate and set our enterprises free.

IN THIS decade, you have undertaken vast new obligations, which we support. But because you have not
applied to these obligations the ordinary standards of
business judgment, you have lost our money by the bil-

lions and we, the people, say: give us a businesslike adminstration that will act as the steward of our prosperity; that will ensure the social progress that is now threatened; that will manage our affairs at least as intelligently as we manage our own enterprises.

IN THIS decade, under the banners of reform, you have usurped our sovereign power by curtailing the Bill of Rights, by short-circuiting the states, and by placing in the hands of a few men in executive commissions all the powers requisite to tyranny; and we, the people, say to you: we do not want monopolistic government, any more than we want monopolistic industry. Give us back the powers that our forefathers declared to be ours; liberate us to govern ourselves by *law*.

BECAUSE you have concealed from us the amount of our real taxes, and because you have hidden from us the real nature of our expenditures, you have specifically usurped our power over the public monies, and we, the people, say: give us as much information concerning our government as we expect to get concerning our own enterprises, so that we may control the vast sums that it has become necessary to spend.

YOU—the politicians of both parties—have muddled our foreign affairs with politics; with vague threats and furtive approvals; with wild fears and inconsistent acts; and we, the people, say: give us a foreign policy that we can trust and upon which we can build toward the future. We are against aggressors; we are for foreign trade; and we recognize that our own standard of living can be improved only by raising the standard of the other countries of the world.

*   *   *

This declaration will not interest those who regard the United States as a laboratory for social experiments.

It will not interest those who regard the United States as a free-lunch counter.

It will certainly not interest those who regard the United States as a somewhat impoverished gold mine out of which they can still scrape a nugget or two for themselves.

It will interest only those who think of the United States as their land—a land that they know and love— a land that became rich through the industry, thrift, and enterprise of its people, and will never regain its prosperity in any other way.

A PLEDGE
TO THE DELEGATES OF
THE REPUBLICAN
CONVENTION

A PLEDGE
TO THE DELEGATES OF THE
REPUBLICAN CONVENTION

An extemporaneous address made on the afternoon of June 28, 1940, to the Republican National Convention at Philadelphia, by Wendell Willkie, in acknowledgment of his selection as the Presidential Nominee of the Republican Party.

A PLEDGE
TO THE DELEGATES OF
THE REPUBLICAN
CONVENTION

By *Wendell Willkie*

I DOUBT if in all the history of American political conventions any convention has ever been presided over with more impartiality, more fairness and more ability than this one has been presided over by Joe Martin.

I want to say to the members of this convention that as your nominee I stand before you without a single pledge, promise or understanding of any kind except for the advancement of your cause and the preservation of American democracy.

It is a moving and appealing and almost overwhelming thing to be the nominee of a great free convention of this kind.

I doubt if any man who has not experienced it could imagine and understand the full import of the emotion it brings when such obligation comes to him.

I wanted to come here to you this afternoon, not to discuss policies or principles, but merely to thank you, to express my appreciation, and to tell you of the deep sense of dedication I feel to the cause that you have asked me to lead.

Democracy, and our way of life, is facing the most crucial test it has ever faced in all its long history; and we are here not as Republicans, alone, but as Americans to dedicate ourselves to the democratic way of life in the United States because here stands the last firm, untouched foothold of freedom in all the world.

As your nominee I expect to conduct a crusading, aggressive, fighting campaign to bring unity to America, to bring the unity of labor and capital, of agriculture and industry, of farmer and worker, the unity of all classes to this great cause of the preservation of freedom.

I think, as one who has been a member of each of those classes in the course of my life, I understand that in America we all have the common purpose at this time that this way of life shall not pass from the earth. For the rehabilitation of American economy; for the building of an adequate defense so that no dictator, however strong, may seek to strike; for the unity of our people; for calling America again to its great tradition of progress, I pledge myself to you, and I ask each of you to join with me in this great crusade.

Forty-eight days ago, and only forty-eight days ago, I started out to preach to the American people the doctrine of unity, the doctrine of the destiny of America, and the fact that I am the nominee of this convention at this time proves conclusively how appealing is this simple doctrine to the American people.

So, Republicans, I call upon you to join me, help me. The cause is great. We must win. We cannot fail if we stand together in one united fight.

And I thank you.

SPEECH OF ACCEPTANCE

SPEECH OF ACCEPTANCE

Delivered at Elwood, Indiana,
on August 17th, 1940.

SPEECH OF ACCEPTANCE

By Wendell Willkie

THE ceremony of an acceptance speech is a tradition
of our pioneer past—before the days of rapid com-
munication. You all know that I accepted at Philadelphia the nomination of the Republican party for
President of the United States. But I take pride in
the traditions and not in change for the mere sake of
overthrowing precedents.

An acceptance speech is a candidate's keynote, a declaration of his broad principles. It cannot possibly
review the issues in detail. I shall, however, cover
each of them frankly during this campaign. Here I
give you an outline of the political philosophy that is
in my heart. We are here today to represent a sacred
cause—the preservation of American democracy.

Obviously, I cannot lead this cause alone. I need
the help of every American—Republican, Democrat or
Independent—Jew, Catholic, or Protestant—people of
every color, creed and race. Party lines are down.
Nothing could make that clearer than the nomination
by the Republicans of a liberal Democrat who changed
his party affiliation because he found democracy in the
Republican party and not in the New Deal party.

And as the leader of the Republican party let me

say this. We go into our campaign as into a crusade. Revitalized and reunited, and joined by millions who share in our cause, we dedicate ourselves to the principles of American liberty, and we shall fight this campaign on the basis of those principles, not on the basis of hate, jealousy, or personalities. The leaders of the Republican party, in Congress and in the party organization, have made me that pledge. I have given that pledge to them. And I extend it to all who will join in this cause. What we need in this country is a new leadership that believes in the destiny of America. I represent here today the forces that will bring that leadership to you.

There is a special reason why I have come back to Elwood, Indiana, to make this acceptance speech. I have an engagement to keep in this town. It was made a long time ago with a young man I knew well.

This young man was born and raised in Elwood. He attended the Elwood public schools. He worked in your factories and stores. He started the practice of law in your courts. As I look back upon him, I realize that he had plenty of faults. But he had also three steadfast convictions. He was devoted to the ideal of individual liberty. He hated all special privileges and forms of oppression. And he knew without any doubt that the greatest country on earth was the United States of America.

That boy was myself thirty or thirty-five years ago. I still adhere to those convictions. To him, to his generation, to his elders, and to the youth of today I pledge my word that I shall never let them down.

In former days America was described as a country in which any young man might become President. It is still that kind of country. The thousands of my fellow townsmen standing hereabout know how distant seemed that opportunity to me thirty years ago. We must fight to preserve America as a country in which every girl and boy has every opportunity for any achievement.

To the millions of our young men and women who have been deliberately disillusioned by the political influences I now oppose; to the millions who no longer believe in the future of their land—to them I want to say in all humility—this boy I knew started like you, without money or position; but America gave him the opportunity for a career. I want to assure a similar opportunity to every boy and girl of today who is willing to stand on his own feet, and work and fight.

I have more reason than most of you to feel strongly about this because the United States gave to my family their first chance for a free life. The ancestors of both my father and my mother, like the ancestors of millions of Americans, lived in Central Europe. They were humble people—not members of the ruling or wealthy classes. Their opportunities were restricted by discriminatory laws and class distinctions. One was exiled because of his religion; another was persecuted because he believed in the principles of the French Revolution; and still another was jailed for insisting on the right of free speech.

As their descendant, I have fought from boyhood against all those restrictions, discriminations and tyrannies. And I am still fighting.

My grandparents lived in Germany. They were supporters of the democratic revolutions in that country, and when the revolutions failed they fled to the United States. How familiar that sounds! Today, also, people are being oppressed in Europe. The story of the barbarous and worse than medieval persecution of the Jews—a race that has done so much to improve the culture of these countries and our own—is the most tragic in human history. Today there are millions of refugees who desire sanctuary and opportunity in America, just as in my grandparents' time. The protection of our own labor and agriculture prevents us from admitting more than a few of them. But their misery and suffering make us resolve to preserve our country as a land free of hate and bitterness, of racial and class distinction. I pledge you that kind of America.

My mother was born in this country. My father was three or four years old when his parents settled in northern Indiana. It was then a trackless forest. As a young man he helped to clear that forest. He worked his way through the Fort Wayne Methodist College, taught school, and became Superintendent of Schools here in Elwood. My mother was also a school teacher. Whenever they had time, they both studied law and eventually both took up the practice of law. I doubt if any two people ever appreciated or loved this country more than they.

As you who lived here with them well know, they were fiercely democratic. They hated oppression, autocracy, or arbitrary control of any kind. They believed in the qualities that have made America great—an independent spirit, an inquiring mind, a courageous heart. At school they taught those virtues to many of you who are here today. At home they taught them to their children. It is a tribute to their teaching that when the United States entered the World War in 1917, three of their four boys were volunteers, in the uniform of the American forces, within one month after war was declared. They withheld no sacrifices for the preservation of the America of 1917. In an even more dangerous world, we must not withhold any sacrifice necessary for the preservation of the America of 1940.

Today we meet in a typical American town. The quiet streets, the pleasant fields that lie outside, the people going casually about their business, seem far removed from the shattered cities, the gutted buildings, and the stricken people of Europe. It is hard for us to realize that the war in Europe can affect our daily lives. Instinctively we turn aside from the recurring conflicts over there, the diplomatic intrigue, the shifts of power that the last war failed to end.

Yet—instinctively also—we know that we are not isolated from those suffering people. We live in the same world as they, and we are created in the same image. In all the democracies that have recently fallen, the people were living the same peaceful lives that we live. They had similar ideals of human freedom. Their methods of trade and exchange were similar to ours. Try as we will, we cannot brush the pitiless picture of their destruction from our vision, or escape the profound effects of it upon the world in which we live.

No man is so wise as to foresee what the future holds or to lay out a plan for it. No man can guarantee to maintain peace. Peace is not something that a nation can achieve by itself. It also depends on what some other country does. It is neither practical, nor desirable, to adopt a foreign program committing the United States to future action under unknown circumstances.

The best that we can do is to decide what principle shall guide us.

For me, that principle can be simply defined:

In the foreign policy of the United States, as in its domestic policy, I would do everything to defend American democracy and I would refrain from doing anything that would injure it.

We must not permit our emotions—our sympathies or hatreds—to move us from that fixed principle.

For instance, we must not shirk the necessity of preparing our sons to take care of themselves in case the defense of America leads to war. I shall not undertake to analyze the legislation on this subject that is now before Congress, or to examine the intentions of the Administration with regard to it. I concur with many members of my party, that these intentions must be closely watched. Nevertheless, in spite of these considerations, I cannot ask the American people to put their faith in me, without recording my conviction that some form of selective service is the only democratic way in which to secure the trained and competent manpower we need for national defense.

Also, in the light of my principle, we must honestly face our relationship with Great Britain. We must admit that the loss of the British Fleet would greatly weaken our defense. This is because the British Fleet has for years controlled the Atlantic, leaving us free to concentrate in the Pacific. If the British Fleet were lost or captured, the Atlantic might be dominated by Germany, a power hostile to our way of life, controlling in that event most of the ships and shipbuilding facilities of Europe.

This would be calamity for us. We might be exposed to attack on the Atlantic. Our defense would be weakened until we could build a navy and air force strong enough to defend both coasts. Also, our foreign trade would be profoundly affected. That trade is vital to our prosperity. But if we had to trade with a Europe dominated by the present German trade policies, we might have to change our methods to some totalitarian form. This is a prospect that any lover of democracy must view with consternation.

The objective of America is in the opposite direction. We must, in the long run, rebuild a world in which we can live and move and do business in the democratic way.

The President of the United States recently said: "We will extend to the opponents of force the material resources of this nation, and at the same time we will harness the use of those resources in order that we ourselves, in the Americas, may have equipment and training equal to the task of any emergency and every defense."

I should like to state that I am in agreement with these two principles, as I understand them—and I don't understand them as implying military involvement in the present hostilities. As an American citizen I am glad to pledge my wholehearted support to the President in whatever action he may take in accordance with these principles.

But I cannot follow the President in his conduct of foreign affairs in this critical time. There have been occasions when many of us have wondered if he is deliberately inciting us to war. I trust that I have made it plain that in the defense of America, and of our liberties, I should not hesitate to stand for war. But like a great many other Americans I saw what war was like at first hand in 1917. I know what war can do to demoralize civil liberties at home. And I believe it to be the first duty of a President to try to maintain peace.

But Mr. Roosevelt has not done this. He has dabbled in inflammatory statements and manufactured panics. Of course, we in America like to speak our minds freely, but this does not mean that at a critical period in history our President should cause bitterness and confusion for the sake of a little political or-

atory.   The President's attacks on foreign powers
have been useless and dangerous.   He has courted a
war for which the country is hopelessly unprepared—
and which it emphatically does not want.   He has
secretly meddled in the affairs of Europe, and he has
even unscrupulously encouraged other countries to
hope for more help than we are able to give.

"Walk softly and carry a big stick" was the motto
of Theodore Roosevelt.   It is still good American doctrine for 1940.   Under the present administration the
country has been placed in the false position of shouting insults and not even beginning to prepare to take
the consequences.

But while he has thus been quick to tell other nations
what they ought to do, Mr. Roosevelt has been slow
to take the American people into his confidence.   He
has hesitated to report facts, to explain situations, or
to define realistic objectives.   The confusion in the
nation's mind has been largely due to this lack of information from the White House.

If I am elected President, I plan to reverse both of
these policies.   I should threaten foreign governments
only when our country was threatened by them and
when I was ready to act; and I should consider our
diplomacy as part of the people's business concerning
which they were entitled to prompt and frank reports
to the limit of practicability.

Candor in these times is the hope of democracy.   We
must not kid ourselves any longer.   We must begin to
tell ourselves the truth—right here—and right now.

We have been sitting as spectators of a great tragedy. The action on the stage of history has been relentless.

For instance, the French people were just as brave and intelligent as the Germans. Their armies were considered the best in the world. France and her allies won the last war. They possessed all the material resources they needed. They had wealth and reserves of credit all over the earth. Yet the Germans crushed France like an eggshell.

The reason is now clear: The fault lay with France herself.

France believed in the forms of democracy and in the idea of freedom. But she failed to put them to use. She forgot that freedom must be dynamic, that it is forever in the process of creating a new world. This was the lesson that we of America had taught to all countries.

When the European democracies lost that vision, they opened the way to Hitler. While Germany was building a great new productive plant, France became absorbed in unfruitful political adventures and flimsy economy theories. Her government was trying desperately to cover the people's nakedness with a garment that was not big enough.

The free men of France should have been weaving themselves a bigger garment. For in trying to pull the small one around themselves they tore it to pieces.

And in this tragedy let us find our lesson. The foreign policy of the United States begins right here in our own land. The first task of our country in its international affairs is to become strong at home. We must regain prosperity, restore the independence of our people, and protect our defensive forces. If that is not done promptly we are in constant danger. If that is done no enemy on earth dare attack us. I propose to do it.

We must face a brutal, perhaps, a terrible fact. Our way of life is in competition with Hitler's way of life.

This competition is not merely one of armaments. It is a competition of energy against energy, production against production, brains against brains, salesmanship against salesmanship.

In facing it we should have no fear. History shows that our way of life is the stronger way. From it has come more wealth, more industry, more happiness, more human enlightenment than from any other way. Free men are the strongest men.

But we cannot just take this historical fact for granted. We must make it live. If we are to out-distance the totalitarian powers, we must arise to a new life of adventure and discovery. We must make a wider horizon for the human race. It is to that new life that I pledge myself.

I promise, by returning to those same American principles that overcame German autocracy once before, both in business and in war, to out-distance Hitler in any contest he chooses in 1940 or after. And I promise that when we beat him, we shall beat him on our own terms, in our own American way.

The promises of the present administration cannot lead you to victory against Hitler, or against anyone else. This administration stands for principles exactly opposite to mine. It does not preach the doctrine of growth. It preaches the doctrine of division. We are not asked to make more for ourselves. We are asked to divide among ourselves that which we already have. The New Deal doctrine does not seek risk, it seeks safety. Let us call it the "I pass" doctrine. The New Deal dealt it, and refused to make any more bets on the American future.

Why, that is exactly the course France followed to her destruction! Like the Blum government in France, so has our government become entangled in unfruitful adventures. As in France, so here, we have heard talk of class distinctions and of economic groups preying upon other groups. We are told that capital hates labor and labor capital. We are told that the different kinds of men, whose task it is to build America, are enemies of one another. And I am ashamed to say that some Americans have made political capital of that supposed enmity.

As for me, I want to say here and now that there is no hate in my heart, and that there will be none in my campaign. It is my belief that there is no hate in the hearts of any group of Americans for any other American group—except as the New Dealers seek to put it there for political purposes. I stand for a new companionship in an industrial society.

Of course, if you start like the New Deal with the

idea that we shall never have many more automobiles or radios, that we cannot develop many new inventions of importance, that our standard of living must remain what it is, the rest of the argument is easy. Since a few people have more than they need and millions have less than they need, it is necessary to redivide the wealth and turn it back from the few to the many.

But this can only make the poor poorer and the rich less rich. It does not really distribute wealth. It distributes poverty.

Because I am a businessman, formerly connected with a large company, the doctrinaires of the opposition have attacked me as an opponent of liberalism. But I was a liberal before many of these men had heard the word, and I fought for many of the reforms of the elder LaFollette, Theodore Roosevelt, and Woodrow Wilson before another Roosevelt adopted—and distorted—liberalism.

I learned my liberalism right here at home. From the factories that came into this town many years ago, large fortunes were made by a few individuals, who thereby acquired too much power over our community. Those same forces were at work throughout the rest of the nation. By 1929 the concentration of private power had gone further than it should ever go in a democracy.

We all know that such concentration of power must be checked. Thomas Jefferson disliked regulation, yet he said that the prime purpose of government in a democracy is to keep men from injuring each other.

We know from our own experience that the less fortunate or less skillful among us must be protected from encroachment. That is why we support what is known as the liberal point of view. That is why we believe in reform.

I believe that the forces of free enterprise must be regulated. I am opposed to business monopolies. I believe in collective bargaining, by representatives of labor's own free choice, without any interference and in full protection of those obvious rights. I believe in the maintenance of minimum standards for wages and of maximum standards for hours. I believe that such standards should constantly improve. I believe in the federal regulation of interstate utilities, of securities markets, and of banking. I believe in federal pensions, in adequate old age benefits, and in unemployment allowances.

I believe that the Federal government has a responsibility to equalize the lot of the farmer, with that of the manufacturer. If this cannot be done by parity of prices, other means must be found—with the least possible regimentation of the farmer's affairs. I believe in the encouragement of cooperative buying and selling, and in the full extension of rural electrification.

The purpose of all such measures is indeed to obtain a better distribution of the wealth and earning power of this country. But I do not base my claim to liberalism solely on my faith in such reforms. American liberalism does not consist merely in reforming things. It consists also in making things.

The ability to grow, the ability to make things, is the measure of man's welfare on this earth. To be free, man must be creative.

I am a liberal because I believe that in our industrial age there is no limit to the productive capacity of any man. And so I believe that there is no limit to the horizon of the United States.

I say that we must substitute for the philosophy of distributed scarcity the philosophy of unlimited productivity. I stand for the restoration of full production and reemployment by private enterprise in America.

And I say that we must henceforth ask certain questions of every reform, and of every law to regulate business or industry. We must ask: Has it encouraged our industries to produce? Has it created new opportunities for our youth? Will it increase our standard of living? Will it encourage us to open up a new and bigger world?

A reform that cannot meet these tests is not a truly liberal reform. It is an "I pass" reform. It does not tend to strengthen our system, but to weaken it. It exposes us to aggressors, whether economic or military. It encourages class distinctions and hatreds. And it will lead us inevitably, as I believe we are now headed, toward a form of government alien to ours, and a way of life contrary to the way that our parents taught us here in Elwood.

It is from weakness that people reach for dictators and concentrated government power. Only the strong can be free.

And only the productive can be strong.

When the present administration came to power in 1933, we heard a lot about the forgotten man. The Government, we were told, must care for those who had no other means of support. With this proposition all of us agreed. And we still hold firmly to the principle that those whom private industry cannot support must be supported by government agency, whether federal or state.

But I want to ask anyone in this audience who is, or has been, on relief whether the support that the Government gives him is enough. Is it enough for the free and able-bodied American to be given a few scraps of cash or credit with which to keep himself and his children just this side of starvation and nakedness? Is that what the forgotten man wanted us to remember?

What that man wanted us to remember was his chance—his right—to take part in our great American adventure.

But this administration never remembered that. It launched a vitriolic and well-planned attack against those very industries in which the forgotten man wanted a chance.

It carried on a propaganda campaign to convince the people that businessmen are iniquitous.

It seized upon its taxing power for political purposes. It has levied taxes to punish one man, to force another to do what he did not want to do, to take a crack at a third whom some government agency disliked, or to promote the experiments of a brain-trust. The direct effect of the New Deal taxes has been to inhibit opportunity. It has diverted the money of the rich from productive enterprises to government bonds, so that the United States treasury—and no one else— may have plenty to spend. Thus, much of the money of the rich is invested in tax-exempt securities.

In this connection let me say that, in its plan for tax revision, the Republican party will follow two simple principles. Taxes shall be levied in accordance with each one's ability to pay. And the primary purpose of levying them will be to raise money. We must—and can—raise more money at less relative cost to the people. We must do it without inflicting on the poor the present disproportionate load of *hidden* taxes.

The New Deal's attack on business has had inevitable results. The investor has been afraid to invest his capital, and therefore billions of dollars now lie idle in the banks. The businessman has been afraid to expand his operations, and therefore millions of men have been turned away from the employment offices. Low incomes in the cities, and irresponsible experiments in the country, have deprived the farmer of his markets.

For the first time in our history, American industry has remained stationary for a decade. It offers no more jobs today than it did ten years ago—and there are 6,000,000 more persons seeking jobs. As a nation of producers we have become stagnant. Much of our industrial machinery is obsolete. And the national standard of living has declined.

It is a statement of fact, and no longer a political accusation, that the New Deal has failed in its program of economic rehabilitation. And the victims of its failures are the very persons whose cause it professes to champion.

The little business men are victims because their chances are more restricted than ever before.

The farmers are victims because many of them are forced to subsist on what is virtually a dole, under centralized direction from Washington.

The nine or ten million unemployed are victims because their chances for jobs are fewer.

Approximately 6,000,000 families are victims because they are on relief.

And unless we do something about it soon, 130,000,000 people—an entire nation—will become victims, because they stand in need of a defense system which this administration has so far proved itself powerless to create anywhere except on paper.

To accomplish these results, the present administration has spent sixty billion dollars.

And I say there must be something wrong with a theory of government or a theory of economics, by which, after the expenditure of such a fantastic sum, we have less opportunity than we had before.

The New Deal believes, as frequently declared, that the spending of vast sums by the government is a vir-

tue in itself.   They tell us that government spending
insures recovery.   Where is the recovery?

The New Deal stands for doing what has to be done
by spending as much money as possible.   I propose to
do it by spending as little money as possible.   This is
one great issue in domestic policy and I propose in this
campaign to make it clear.

And I make this grave charge against this administration:

I charge that the course this administration is following will lead us, like France, to the end of the road.
I say that this course will lead us to economic disinte-
gration and dictatorship.

I say that we must substitute for the philosophy of
spending, the philosophy of production.   You cannot
buy freedom.   You must make freedom.

This is a serious charge.   It is not made lightly.
And it cannot be lightly avoided by the opposition.

I, therefore, have a proposal to make.

The President stated in his acceptance speech that
he does not have either "the time or the inclination to
engage in purely political debate."   I do not want to
engage in purely political debate, either.   But I believe that the tradition of face to face debate is justly
honored among our American political traditions.   I
believe that we should set an example, at this time, of
the workings of American democracy.   And I do not
think that the issues at stake are "purely political."   In
my opinion they concern the life and death of democracy.

I propose that during the next two and a half months, the President and I appear together on public platforms in various parts of the country, to debate the fundamental issues of this campaign. These are the problems of our great domestic economy, as well as of our national defense: The problems of agriculture, of labor, of industry, of finance, of the government's relationship to the people, and of our preparations to guard against assault. And also I should like to debate the question of the assumption by this President, in seeking a third term, of a greater public confidence than was accorded to our presidential giants, Washington, Jefferson, Jackson, Lincoln, Cleveland, Theodore Roosevelt, and Woodrow Wilson.

I make this proposal respectfully to a man upon whose shoulders rest the cares of the state. But I make it in dead earnest.

I accept the nomination of the Republican party for President of the United States.

I accept it in the spirit in which I know it was given at our convention in Philadelphia—the spirit of dedication. I herewith dedicate myself with all my heart, with all my mind, and with all my soul to making this nation strong.

But I say this, too. In the pursuit of that goal I shall not lead you down the easy road. If I am chosen the leader of this democracy as I am now of the Republican party, I shall lead you down the road of sacrifice and of service to your country.

What I am saying is a far harsher thing than I should like to say in this speech of acceptance—a far harsher thing than I would have said had the old world not been swept by war during the past year. I am saying to you that we cannot rebuild our American democracy without hardship, without sacrifice, even— without suffering. I am proposing that course to you as a candidate for election by you.

When Winston Churchill became Prime Minister of England a few months ago, he made no sugar-coated promises. "I have nothing to offer you," he said, "but blood, tears, toil, and sweat." Those are harsh words, brave words; yet if England lives, it will be because her people were told the truth and accepted it. Fortunately, in America, we are not reduced to "blood and tears." But we shall not be able to avoid the "toil and sweat."

In these months ahead of us, every man who works in this country—whether he works with his hands or with his mind—will have to work a little harder. Every man and woman will feel the burden of taxes. Every housewife will have to plan a little more carefully. I speak plainly because you must not be deceived about the difficulties of the future. You will have to be hard of muscle, clear of head, brave of heart.

Today great institutions of freedom, for which humanity has spilled so much blood, lie in ruins. In Europe those rights of person and property—the civil liberties—which your ancestors fought for, and which you still enjoy, are virtually extinct. And it is my profound conviction that even here in this country, the Democratic party, under its present leadership, will prove incapable of protecting those liberties of yours.

The Democratic party today stands for division among our people; for the struggle of class against class and faction against faction; for the power of political machines and the exploitation of pressure groups. Liberty does not thrive in such soil.

The only soil in which liberty can grow is that of a united people. We must have faith that the welfare of one is the welfare of all. We must know that the truth can only be reached by the expression of our free opinions, without fear and without rancor. We must acknowledge that all are equal before God and before the law. And we must learn to abhor those disruptive pressures, whether religious, political, or economic, that the enemies of liberty employ.

The Republican party and those associated with it, constitute a great political body that stands preeminently for liberty—without commitments, without fear, and without contradictions. This party believes that your happiness must be achieved through liberty rather than in spite of liberty. We ask you to turn your eyes upon the future, where your hope lies. We see written there the same promise that has always been written there: the promise that strong men will perform strong deeds.

With the help of Almighty Providence, with unyielding determination and ceaseless effort, we must and we shall make that American promise come true.